Youth Retreats

Creating Sacred Space
for Young People

Youth Retreats

Creating Sacred Space
for Young People

Aileen A.
Doyle

Saint Mary's Press
Christian Brothers Publications
Winona, Minnesota

*To my family—Mom, Dad, Jim, Michael,
Mary Catherine, Joe, and Martha*

The publishing team for this book included Rev. Robert
P. Stamschror, editor; Barbara Allaire, manuscript editor;
Mary Kraemer, production editor; Carolyn Thomas,
designer.

Front cover photos: James L. Shaffer (left, middle) and
Jean-Claude Lejeune (right). Back cover photo: James
L. Shaffer. The photos on pages 13, 39, and 73 are by
James L. Shaffer.

The acknowledgments continue on page 8.

Printed in the United States of America

Printing—sixth fifth fourth third second
        1993 92 91 90 89 88 87

ISBN 0-88489-177-1

Contents

Foreword

Those of us who have labored in the ministry of student retreats continue to be fascinated by the movement of the Spirit in retreat programs and personnel. While goals and methodologies vary, the programs have been successful because we, as retreat leaders, have temporarily set aside our own needs and concerns and have dedicated ourselves to the service of the retreatants. We have provided an experience of Christian community for young men and women, where their intellectual knowledge could be integrated with their spiritual and emotional selves. The student retreatants have experienced the love and understanding of God, family, friends, and self as they live out their faith in the unique retreat atmosphere of interaction and reflection. Retreat personnel are instruments of the Spirit, and their dedication and generous service give testimony to the Christian faith.

There are thousands of excellent retreat programs, each with its own merits and distinctions. I have yet to see one in which the retreatants expressed anything but satisfaction. Methods vary but the results are the same. No program should be so sacred that it can't be changed or adapted. Retreat personnel have been consciously and unconsciously learning from each other for many years. Retreat activities, programs, ideas, and experiences thought to be original and unique to one retreat center or geographical area "miraculously" appear in other centers and programs thousands of miles away. We have learned from the gifts and from the experiences of talented retreat personnel over the years. There is little in retreat programming that hasn't been borrowed or shared.

In this retreat manual, Aileen Doyle has given us many time-tested recipes for retreat success. Her organizational skills and creative gifts provide ideas, suggestions, and practical details for effective retreat ministry. Aileen has shared her own creative programs as well as programs that are the result of many years of "fine-tuning." After reading, studying, and reflecting upon these retreat programs, select and/or adapt those parts that will be most helpful to your retreatants. May the prayerful consideration of these pages by your retreat team inspire your programs and retreatants. I pray that Aileen's astute insights into the philosophy and the design of student retreats will enable you to be more effective instruments of the Holy Spirit in the service of youth.

Bro. Kenneth Biggs, FSC
Administrator
Christian Brothers' Retreat House
Saint Helena, California
1 July 1985

Preface

In 1982, I was fortunate to learn of the Christian Brothers' Retreat House in Saint Helena, California. Since 1974, I had worked as a college admissions counselor, a high school coach (volleyball and tennis), a high school teacher (religion and mathematics), and a coordinator for a retreat program in a high school. I enjoyed being with the teenagers.

I found, however, that the structure of the school setting seldom gave the teenagers the opportunity to *reflect* seriously upon their personal beliefs and experiences—something they are very capable of and *want* to do. Research has shown that at puberty the highest level of abstract thinking first makes an appearance. The ability to reason inductively and deductively is new to the adolescent and represents a normal stage of growth. This development takes place at the same time that many adolescents rebel against and withdraw from adults and their values.

To foster this reflective skill, besides presenting traditional doctrine in my high school religion classes, I began to invite the students to offer their own questions and beliefs. I discovered an honest search and a desire to know the truth. As I trusted this searching process and the integrity of the adolescent students, I found that their trust for me increased. The students offered very little resistance when I presented the Christian tradition, because they were given the opportunity to seriously reflect upon and react to the presented material. Most often adolescents rechoose the values of their parents after going through a "letting go" stage. I allowed the students to have the space to "let go" in order to be able to "reown" the values discussed.

In 1982, I began to work at the Christian Brothers' Retreat House. As a staff of eight men and women who live together in Christian community at the retreat house, we provide fifty student retreats each year for over two thousand retreatants. Some of these retreats include programs for teenagers with their parents. All of the retreat programs have evolved over the years.

The retreat house was established in 1962 by the California District of the Institute of the Brothers of Christian Schools (commonly called the Christian Brothers). It originally served as an extension of the religion departments of several high schools operated by the Brothers. During the past ten years, the retreat house has expanded its services to offer programs for over twenty-one high schools located in California and in Oregon. The programs evolved from the preached, quiet retreats of the 1960s and the encounter-type retreats of the 1970s into a style that fits the needs of today's young people. The staff members continually listen to the needs of the young retreatants and try to provide programs that meet those needs.

The goal of the current programs is to create a safe place where the Lord can speak to the young retreatants. Underlying this goal is the assumption that the staff member does not necessarily know what the Lord wants to say to an individual retreatant. The Lord speaks through nature, Scripture, other people, and experiences. As a staff, we are not hesitant to present fundamental Catholic teaching. The manner in which we trust, invite, and challenge the retreatants is the key to their receptiveness. The staff members provide the atmosphere and the tools, and the retreatants do the work. We trust that the Spirit is able to work through us and the program.

Four of the retreats presented in this book have been used as programs at the Christian Brothers' Retreat House. These include Retreat 5 ("Values"), Retreat 7 ("Parent-Teen Relationships"—overnight version), Retreat 8 ("Journey"), and Retreat 9 ("Parent-Teen Relationships"—weekend version). The basic flow of these retreats was designed by past staff members of the retreat house.

The other six retreats are on themes that I believe address the needs of the adolescents as well as the current world situation. These include four one-day retreats ("Called to Be a Follower of Jesus," "Confirmation," "Vocation," and "Christian Conscience Formation"), one overnight retreat ("Prayer"), and one weekend retreat ("Peacemakers").

Acknowledgments

I wish to thank my parents, who worked hard to see that I had a strong foundation in religious education in the Roman Catholic tradition.

I would also like to thank the retreatants, the staff members, and the friends of the Christian Brothers' Retreat House who have influenced the development of these retreats. The current administrator, Bro. Kenneth Biggs, has supported me tremendously in this project.

And finally, I thank the students, the faculty, and the administration of Our Lady of Providence High School in Clarksville, Indiana. It was there, from 1979 to 1982, that my students taught me how to listen to and enjoy the company of teenagers.

I wish also to acknowledge the following permissions to use material previously published or authorized.

The "Attributes of Jesus" list on Handout 1–A in chapter 1 was authored by Sr. Julie Weckwerth. Used by permission.

The scriptural excerpt on Handout 3–B in chapter 3 is from the New American Bible. Copyright 1970 by the Catholic Press and The Confraternity of Christian Doctrine, Washington, D.C., 1970. Used by permission.

The scriptural excerpt on Handout 6–A in chapter 6 is from the Good News Bible, the Bible in Today's English Version. Copyright 1976 by American Bible Society, New York. Used by permission.

The "Uniqueness Prayer" on Handout 7–A in chapter 7 was authored by Andre Auw. Used by permission.

Introduction

Creating a Space

Each retreat presented in this book is intended to create a space where the teenaged retreatant and the Lord can come together. Often the staff members do not have a clue as to whether or not this coming together is actually happening during the retreat. In spite of this lack of visible evidence, it is imperative that the staff members do not lose sight of their role and that they continue to trust the work of the Holy Spirit.

Some inexperienced and overly zealous staff members have a tendency to get in the way of the process by forcing issues, by trying to solve all of the retreatants' problems, or by trying to make their "own" retreat during the time set aside for the retreatants. Forcing issues only makes the retreatants resistant. Trying to solve the retreatants' problems often gives them the message that they are not capable of making their own decisions. Staff members who use the retreat as their own time for reflection are not able to fully tune in to the specific needs of the teenaged retreatants. This goal of creating a space and an atmosphere of trust must be understood by the adults chosen to staff these retreats; their attitudes should reflect this goal.*

Each retreat presented here is designed with the assumption that the retreatants have had and/or are currently receiving religious education. Because of this assumption, the retreats are not based on lectures. In each program the retreatants are invited and encouraged to explore their beliefs, attitudes, and questions. The retreat is a safe place for this exploration. At the same time, the retreatants need to be challenged to examine various sides of an issue, to listen to other perspectives and experiences, and to continue their search for the truth.

Each staff member has the responsibility to work within his or her own professional limits. This includes encouraging the retreatants to participate to the best of their abilities, affirming the retreatants' self-worth, and suggesting problem-solving skills when necessary. But there are times when a retreatant needs to be referred to a counselor or a therapist for professional help. Retreatants who need such help include those dealing with any of the following issues: abortion; alcohol or drug addiction; anorexia nervosa; extreme depression; severe family problems; pregnancy; suicidal thoughts; and physical, sexual, or mental abuse. These issues should be addressed privately and not discussed in the small group as a group therapy session. If such an issue does come up in the small group, confidentiality should be stressed to the members of the group.

Ten retreat programs are presented. There are four one-day retreats, three overnight retreats, and three weekend retreats. For each retreat the following sections are presented: (*a*) goals, (*b*) schedule, (*c*) retreat activities, and (*d*) what to consider before the retreat. The section on retreat activities includes instructions for the activities, scripts to be adapted by the retreat staff, and suggestions that will contribute to the smooth running of a program. The section on what to consider before the retreat covers advance details, personnel needed, an agenda for the staff preretreat planning meeting, and materials needed, including handouts. For information or suggestions that are common to several retreats, the reader of a given retreat is referred to another part of the manual—to this introduction, to one of the other retreats, or to the Appendix.

The designs presented here need to be considered and adapted in light of the facilities being used, the personalities of the retreatants, and the personal styles and experiences of the staff members. I encourage others to be creative in working with these retreats.

Tips for Successful Retreats

The staff should be flexible with the schedule and the activities during the retreat. Below are some suggestions that we have found helpful in our retreats. They can be used depending upon the needs of a particular group.

Details at the Retreat

Icebreakers: See "Resources" on p. 108 for books that have suggestions for icebreakers, in addition to those suggested within the retreat descriptions.

---

*In his book *Adolescent Spirituality,* Charles Shelton, SJ, offers a list of ten questions for youth ministers to prayerfully reflect on. The questions cover areas such as the motivation, the support, and the prayer life of the minister. I highly recommend this book to veterans of youth ministry, as well as to anyone new to the field who works with the programs in this book.

Introductions: A slide presentation about the retreat facility can be prepared to help orient the retreatants to the facility.

Chapel: The chapel is an ideal location for the introduction and prayer at the beginning of the retreat, as well as for the other prayer services and the liturgy.

Breaks: During each break the staff should take turns supervising the retreatants. The dorm should be a restricted area when unsupervised. This discourages practical jokes in the rooms. The dorm should always be a place of quiet.

Cleanup: Most retreat facilities expect the retreatants to remake the beds and clean the rooms. Time is set aside for this on the overnight retreats. It is helpful to prepare slides to show the retreatants how to make the beds, where to empty the trash, and how to carry out any other expectations regarding cleanup.

Closedown: In order to keep a large group in control, ask all the retreatants on the overnight and weekend retreats to have their lights out twenty minutes after the last activity ends. Discourage them from using the showers until the morning. Suggest writing in their journals as a way to unwind in the late evening before retiring.

Discipline: When rules have been broken by a few people (for example, trashing the dorm), call the whole group together. Name the inappropriate behavior. Ask for assistance with any tasks that might be needed, such as cleaning up the area. Refocus the retreatants by reminding them of the theme of the retreat. Ask for cooperation and state the consequences you intend to give for any more inappropriate behavior. Move on to the next retreat activity.

Emergencies: In the event of a medical emergency, a staff member should accompany the retreatant to the doctor's office or to the hospital. Call the parents immediately, and call the school if this is a school-sponsored activity.

Wake-up music: Play semi-mellow music on a tape player.

Liturgy: In the event that a eucharistic liturgy is not possible or is not the best option, celebrate with a Communion service. Such a service begins with the penitential rite, moves on to the liturgy of the Word, and concludes with the Communion rite. The retreatants on the overnight and weekend retreats should still plan the readings, the petitions, the decorations, and the music.

Meals: Have the retreatants stay in the dining room until any announcements have been made. Have an adult available to supervise the cleaning of tables as well as to supervise the recreational areas.

Memento cards: A nice touch is to give the retreatants a memento card from the retreat. The card could have printed on it the date, the location, and the theme of the retreat, with a quote from Scripture (for example, First Corinthians, chapter 13) or the Peace Prayer attributed to Saint Francis (see Handout 10–A). Some retreatants request a list of the scriptural passages used throughout the retreat.

Organized recreation: If the weather is poor and the retreatants are not able to play any organized games outside, use some icebreakers from the book *New Games* (see "Resources" on p. 108).

Reconciliation: In the event that celebration of the Sacrament of Penance is not possible or is not the best option, invite the retreatants to come to a staff member to pray together for forgiveness or to simply talk about a particular concern.

Schedules: Times are flexible. In retreats with a large number of participants, the activities tend to take more time than in retreats with fewer participants. Rearrange the times suggested on the schedule, noting that the retreat house's mealtimes must be respected for the sake of the kitchen staff. Post the schedule in the dorm, the dining room, and the recreational areas. This is another way to encourage the retreatants to take the responsibility to be on time for each activity.

Concretizing: Announce the date of any scheduled follow-up meeting. Gather the group for a picture.

Large-Group Presentations

Preparation: Don't attempt to "wing it." Preparing well will build your confidence and make your talk more convincing.

Organization: Use a basic outline and notes. These can be put on index cards. Include an introduction, a clear message, a summary, and a conclusion.

Volume: Project your voice with adequate volume.

Directions: Give directions for activities *twice.* Speak slowly and include expectations and boundaries.

Reacting: Try not to overreact to retreatants' behaviors or comments that seem inappropriate.

Attending: Make eye contact with the retreatants. Try to be aware of what else is going on in the room. Do not ignore problems.

Humor: Control your humor. Use it moderately in a large group, as it is difficult to regain the control of the group once it is lost. (Some inexperienced staff members joke around with the retreatants and then become frustrated if the retreatants do not refocus immediately.)

Simplicity: Do not confuse the retreatants with too many ideas. It is better for them to remember one good idea than to forget six.

Experience: Use words and symbols that touch the retreatants' experiences.

Moralizing: Avoid "You should . . ." messages. Very few of us are willing to listen to such moralizing. It is doubtful that teenaged retreatants will listen to it either.

Small-Group Facilitation

Seating: For a relaxed atmosphere that is conducive to discussion and eye contact, arrange the chairs for each small group in a circle.

Respect for space: Protect the psychological space of each individual. The small groups are not therapy groups for the purpose of personality dissection ("Are you comfortable answering that question?").

Sensitivity: Sense the moods of the retreatants (e.g., restless, tired, anxious, hopeful) and try to respond appropriately. If you don't know how they are feeling, ask them ("What are some of your feelings as you sit here?").

Variety of needs: Be aware of the retreatant who lacks confidence and needs to be invited to speak ("Is there something you would like to add about what has been said?"), as well as the retreatant who is content and needs to be left alone.

Steering: Deflect discussions that sidetrack the group. Give a gentle halt to one who dominates ("Let's hear from those of you who have not said anything yet").

Humor: Use humor; it is easier to deal with in a small group than a large group. Keep it light, reflecting a positive outlook, *not* sarcasm or ridicule.

Being "right": Don't ask questions that imply you are always right ("Don't you see that you are wrong?").

Feedback: Make your feedback prompt and accurate ("You are nodding. Does that mean that you agree?").

Reacting: React to the message itself, not the methods of the person speaking. Some retreatants have poor communication skills; they might "attack" your ideas. Respond to their words, not their style. Continue to affirm their search for truth.

Openness: Trust. Listen. Affirm.

Language: When appropriate, point out to the retreatants that certain forms of the language enhance personal awareness. Try to use these forms yourself:
- pronoun changes—*we* to *I; you* to *I; it* to *I*
- verb changes—*can't* to *won't; need* to *want; have to* to *choose to; know* to *imagine*
- questions—*how* and *what* instead of *why*

What to Consider Before the Retreat

Before the retreat, the leaders need to consider planning details, the personnel needed, the agenda for the staff preretreat planning meeting, and the materials needed.

Details in Advance

Timing: Make preparations well in advance.

Facilities: Check the retreat facilities for conference rooms, a chapel, small-group rooms, the number of bedrooms, recreational facilities, vending machines, mealtimes and menus, and costs.

Letter to parents: Compose a suitable letter to the parents of the potential retreatants informing them of the value of the experience.

Sign-ups: Conduct sign-ups for the dates. Ask for a nonrefundable deposit to hold the retreatant's place.

Deposit: Send a deposit to the retreat house.

Arrangements with priest: Make arrangements with the priest who will celebrate the sacraments for the dates and the times he will be needed.

Medical forms: Collect signed medical release and permission forms from each retreatant, to be used in case of emergency.

Dorm list: Prepare a dorm list, giving special attention to those who may need to share a room.

Medical supplies: Gather supplies of antibiotic ointment, bandages, cotton balls, alcohol, aspirin, allergy tablets, cough syrup, remedy for poison oak and poison ivy, antacid tablets, tweezers, needles, ice pack, feminine sanitary napkins, and tampons.

Play equipment: Gather recreational equipment such as playing cards, basketballs, volleyballs, table tennis balls and paddles, footballs, and Frisbees.

Damages: Be aware that you are responsible for reimbursing the retreat house for any damages caused by carelessness or misconduct.

Staff preretreat planning meeting: Arrange for a meeting with the staff who will be giving the retreat as a team (see "Agenda for the Staff Preretreat Planning Meeting" on p. 12).

Meeting with retreatants: Meet with the retreatants before the retreat to go over details.

1. The theme of the retreat
2. What to bring
   - clothing—casual, warm
   - music—musical instruments (no tape players)
   - books—selective reading books (no homework)
   - medicine—any required prescription medications
3. Expectations
   - Punctuality is expected for the smooth running of the retreat.
   - Retreatants are expected to respect the privacy of each person's bedroom.
   - The use of drugs or alcohol is prohibited.
   - All retreatants are expected to be present for all retreat activities and are expected to participate to the degree that they are comfortable.
4. Collection of payments due
5. Time and place of departure
6. Travel arrangements (If some retreatants are driving, pass out maps. Have a list of the names of the drivers and the passengers in each car.)
7. Questions from the retreatants
8. Encouragement of prayer for the success of their retreat

Personnel Needed

Recommended number of adults: We advise that there be one adult for each ten retreatants, another to coordinate the retreat activities, and two more to share supervision responsibilities. At the least, the retreat should be staffed by one adult for each ten retreatants.

Note: The adults are responsible for facilitating the small-group discussions, as well as for leading large-group activities. One of the adults should be a priest or an adult capable of presiding at a Communion service.

Agenda for the Staff Preretreat Planning Meeting

1. Prayer: Open the planning meeting with prayer, asking for the grace needed to create a space where the retreatants will be open to meeting the Lord during their retreat.

2. Needs of the retreatants: Notify the staff about any medical problems that might arise during the retreat (e.g., asthma, allergies). Discuss pertinent facts about the retreatants' school activities or family situations (e.g., final exams, recent death in the family).

Some of the above problems may surface in the small-group discussions. It is helpful for the group facilitator to be aware of these problems ahead of time, in order to be more sensitive to the needs of the small-group members. This part of the meeting is *not* meant to be a time to gossip or pass on stereotyped images of the retreatants.

3. Small groups: Decide on the size (between six and ten retreatants) and the composition of the small groups and assign the retreatants to these groups while
- balancing boys and girls,
- separating any couples or pairs who would inhibit the freedom of others in the group, and
- balancing the talkative and quiet retreatants within each group.

4. Staff responsibilities: Decide which staff members will lead each activity. Be sensitive to the need to share the responsibilities. This distribution of tasks helps to conserve the energy that is needed for quality presentations and small-group facilitating.

5. Transportation: Decide upon and arrange the transportation (bus or cars). Make sure maps are available for the staff members and/or retreatants who are driving.

6. Liturgy planning: For the one-day retreats, use this time in the agenda to select the readings and songs for the liturgy (suggested readings are provided for each one-day retreat in this manual). For the overnight and weekend retreats, the retreatants will plan the liturgy during the retreat by working in committees, so use this time to go over the arrangements for assisting them in their tasks (see the Appendix on pp. 103–107, "Eucharistic Liturgy Preparation for Overnight and Weekend Retreats").

Materials Needed

Lists: a roster for arrival, an alphabetical list of retreatants' names (one for each staff member), and a list of membership of each small group (one for each staff member)

Paper and writing supplies: index cards, a roll of butcher paper or a pad of newsprint, 8½-by-11-inch paper, pencils, and felt-tip markers

Materials for liturgy: a chalice, a plate, bread, wine, water, a corporal, a purificator, a candle, matches, a Bible, the Sacramentary, music books, and copies of the program

Miscellaneous: stick-on name tags, a camera and film, a tape recorder and tapes, a roll of masking tape for each small group, and recreational equipment (e.g., volleyballs, Frisbees, football)

Additional items to bring will be listed in "Materials needed" at the end of each retreat. Necessary handouts are also listed in that section of each retreat. The handout "Planning Sheet for Eucharistic Liturgy," which is on page 107 in the Appendix, can be reproduced and used for all retreats.

Part A
One-Day Retreats

Retreat 1 ("Called to Be a Follower of Jesus"), the first of the four one-day retreats, is meant to be used with younger (eighth-, ninth-, and tenth-grade) retreatants. The retreatants reflect upon their call to be followers of Jesus. The program provides the retreatants with an opportunity to examine their attitudes and beliefs. It is assumed that they have had previous religious education. This retreat can be used as a mandatory program.

Retreat 2 ("Confirmation") is meant to be used with high school-aged retreatants who are preparing to be confirmed. The retreatants prepare to confirm their faith by taking time to examine their beliefs. It is assumed that the retreatants are currently participating in instructions for Confirmation.

Retreat 3 ("Vocation") is meant to be used with older (eleventh- and twelfth-grade) retreatants. The program provides the retreatants with the opportunity to reflect upon their attitudes toward certain lifestyles in the Christian tradition, as well as to examine their understanding of their personal vocations. It is assumed that the retreatants have freely chosen to attend this program.

Retreat 4 ("Christian Conscience Formation") is meant to be used with older (tenth-, eleventh-, and twelfth-grade) retreatants. The retreatants reflect upon ways to form and nurture a Christian conscience. It is assumed that the retreatants have freely chosen to attend this program.

For each retreat, arrangements for lunch need to be made ahead of time. Either the retreatants bring a sack lunch and the staff provides the drinks, or the retreat facility provides the lunch. If the retreatants bring their own lunches, be sure to provide trash bags. Snacks (cookies, popcorn, punch) are popular treats. It seems the retreatants' appetites increase when they are away from home for the day.

Mandatory retreats often need more adult supervision. Retreats 1 and 2 are designed to accommodate retreatants who are required to take part in the program, whereas Retreats 3 and 4 are designed for retreatants who have freely chosen to attend. Resistance from the retreatants would make it particularly difficult for these two programs to be effective.

Retreat 1
Called to Be a Follower of Jesus

Goals

The retreat "Called to Be a Follower of Jesus" is designed for younger (eighth-, ninth-, and tenth-grade) retreatants. It is a single-day program for twenty to forty participants.

The goals of the retreat are the following:

1. Through Scripture and prayer, the retreatants will look at their call to be followers of Jesus.
2. The retreatants will articulate their beliefs about Jesus and hear other retreatants' beliefs.
3. The retreatants will examine ways that they might follow Jesus more closely in their daily living.

Schedule

9:00 a.m.	Arrival
9:15 a.m.	Introduction and prayer
9:45 a.m.	Icebreakers
10:30 a.m.	Small group 1
11:30 a.m.	Large group
12:00 m.	Lunch
12:30 p.m.	Organized recreation
1:00 p.m.	Quiet time
1:30 p.m.	Small group 2
2:45 p.m.	Liturgy
3:45 p.m.	Concretizing
4:00 p.m.	Departure

Retreat Activities

9:00 a.m. Arrival

Two staff members welcome and register the retreatants and have them fill out name tags.

9:15 a.m. Introduction and prayer

Staff: two people

Purposes: to lead the retreat community in prayer, to introduce the theme of the retreat, to introduce the retreat staff, and to explain guidelines for using the retreat facility

Materials needed: a Bible

Description of activities

Part 1: "Welcome to your retreat. My name is _____. As we begin this day, I invite you to take a moment to quietly call upon Jesus to speak to you today." Pause.

"Your retreat today focuses on your call to be a follower of Jesus. Many teenagers whom I have met think that they are too young to be followers of Jesus. I would like to read to you a passage from the book of Jeremiah. He, too, felt that he was too young to speak for the Lord." Read Jer. 1:4–8.

"At times we are just like Jeremiah saying to the Lord, 'I don't know how to speak. I am too young.' Yet the Lord reassures Jeremiah that he will place the words in Jeremiah's mouth at the appropriate time. I challenge you today to be open to the ways Jesus wants to speak through you. I believe that each of us is called to follow Jesus by loving as he taught us to love. One of the last things Jesus said to his friends was, 'Love one another as I have loved you' [John 15:12].

"During this retreat you will have a chance to look at your views about Jesus. You will have a chance to examine how you spend your time and what you do with the things that are important to you. In order to follow Jesus more closely, are there any areas that need to be changed in your life?

"I invite you to try to set a goal for yourself for this retreat. Is there something that you would like to work toward during the next six hours? In order for you to get the most out of this retreat experience, I encourage you to take the responsibility to fully participate in each activity. As you set your goal, be sure to ask Jesus to assist you." Pause.

Part 2: "There are some people that I would like you to meet now. They are here to help create the atmosphere and the space for you to do the work during this retreat." Introduce individually each staff member. It is helpful if they say something about themselves so that the retreatants can get to know them a little better.

"Now that you know who we are, I want to explain to you some practical details about using this retreat facility:

- Whenever you are in the chapel, please have your behavior reflect the reverence appropriate for the house of the People of God. Note that the sanctuary lamp burns as a reminder that Jesus is present to us in a very special way in the Eucharist, which is reserved in the tabernacle.
- Please wear your name tags throughout the retreat. It helps us to get to know one another's names.
- The restrooms are located _____.
- If you need any medical supplies, please see ____ _____.
- Please try to be on time for each activity. Normally, we will not begin an activity unless everyone is present.
- If there is any way that we can assist you, please feel free to ask any of the staff members.

"I want to remind you again that the success of this retreat depends upon each of you giving your best effort. We look forward to working with you. Throughout the retreat we will continue to pray for you.

"At this time we would like you to go to _____ _____ [location of the icebreaker activity] so that we can begin our icebreakers."

9:45 a.m. Icebreakers

Staff: one person

Purpose: to help the retreatants feel more at ease with one another

Materials needed: none

Description of activities

1. Birth dates: Have the retreatants stand and form one large circle by lining up in the order of the month in which their birth date falls. Begin with January. After they have formed the circle, ask them to call out in order the date of their birth. Stress cooperation and listening during this activity.

2. Music: Tell the retreatants to stand and form one large circle by lining up in alphabetical order according to the first letter of the name of each person's favorite musical entertainer or musical group. After they have formed the circle, ask them to call out in turn the name of their favorite musician or group. Stress acceptance during this activity.

3. Knots: Divide the group into two circles. The retreatants should note who is standing on their right and left. Give both groups fifteen seconds to mingle among their respective circle members. After fifteen seconds, call, "Freeze." Tell the retreatants to reach out and take the hands of the people who originally stood on their right and left. After the group is holding hands, challenge them to try to "untie" the knot without letting go of any clasped hands. If there are less than twenty retreatants, do not split the group into two circles.

4. Summary: After the icebreakers, have the retreatants sit. Talk a little about the cooperation, listening, acceptance, and participation by all that were needed for the icebreakers to be a success. Remind them that these same skills are important for the entire retreat and specifically during the small-group meetings. Assign small groups and explain the location of the meeting rooms.

10:30 a.m. Small group 1

Staff: one person for each small group

Purposes: to assist the retreatants in establishing small-group discussion rules, to encourage the retreatants to set personal goals for the retreat, and to have them reflect on and discuss the attributes of Jesus that mean the most to them

Materials needed for each group: an 8½-by-11-inch paper and a pencil for each retreatant; Handout 1–A, "Attributes of Jesus"; a roll of masking tape; a large piece of butcher paper; and a felt-tip marker

Description of activities

1. Introduction (10 min.): "Let's begin with some simple introductions. As we go around the circle, please tell us your name and the reason why you decided to attend this retreat." Have each person introduce himself or herself, and encourage the others to respond in some way.

2. Guidelines (5 min.): "Before we go on with our activity, let's establish some guidelines for discussion. What makes a good discussion happen? I will write down the guidelines you suggest and hang them on the wall so we can refer to them if necessary."

With a felt-tip marker, write the guidelines on the butcher paper. Make sure the following are included: confidentiality, respect, no put-downs, honesty, and an attempt to participate by all.

3. Personal goals (5 min.): "What is a goal you could set for yourself for the retreat? What do you need in your life at this time?" Pass out pencils and paper. Ask the retreatants to write a personal goal on the paper.

4. Attributes of Jesus activity (30 min.): Distribute Handout 1–A, "Attributes of Jesus." "At this time I would like to give you a chance to examine some of your beliefs about Jesus. You have been taught many things. What means a lot to you? If we are to follow Jesus, I think that it is very important to look at who he really is.

"Carefully read the list of the attributes of Jesus. Think about each one. Choose the five attributes that mean the most to you. Circle them and rank them in the order of their importance to you."

Invite the retreatants to discuss their choices with the other group members. Encourage all to participate. Make sure the guidelines are observed. If the group is timid, pair each retreatant with another person for a two-minute dyad. Then return to the group discussion. After twenty minutes, have the group come to a consensus on the five most important attributes of Jesus. List these on the butcher paper. Have the group choose a spokesperson to report to the large group. Make sure the spokesperson understands why the group chose the selected attributes.

5. Closure: End with a closing prayer and invite the retreatants to go to the room designated for the large-group activity.

11:30 a.m. Large group

Staff: one person

Purpose: to pull together the opinions and feelings shared in the small groups

Materials needed: a large piece of butcher paper, a felt-tip marker, and a roll of masking tape

Description of activities
1. Reports: Invite the representatives from each small group to report the consensus they reached on the five most important attributes of Jesus. Hang the papers on the wall so that all are able to read them. After each explanation is given, encourage the large group to ask clarifying questions of the group's representative.

2. Process: Review the attributes of Jesus that were selected by the groups. Have the retreatants give examples of times when Jesus actually lived out these attributes. Ask them to give examples of times when they might be able to live out these attributes themselves.

3. Consensus: Invite the large group to come to a consensus on what they think the five most important attributes of Jesus are. List these on a piece of butcher paper.

4. Closure: Thank the retreatants for their honesty, cooperation, and trust in one another. Dismiss the group for lunch.

12:00 m. Lunch

One staff person is available to make announcements and to choose a retreatant to lead the group in prayer before the meal.

12:30 p.m. Organized recreation

Staff: two people

Purpose: to have the retreatants experience exercise and fun as a group

Materials needed: recreational equipment (e.g., two volleyballs, footballs, basketballs, Frisbees)

1:00 p.m. Quiet time

Staff: two people to supervise the retreatants

Purpose: to introduce the value of reflection through quiet time spent alone

Materials needed: a slide projector, a screen, appropriate slides (e.g., of nature or of people helping others), a tape recorder, and an appropriate tape

Description of activities
"I find it important in my life to take time from my busy schedule in order to reflect on how I am following Jesus. At the times when I reflect on this, I also remind myself of Jesus' message by reading the Scriptures. Jesus' message is to love as he did. I look in the Gospels to see the ways that he did love others. He forgave people when others did not think they should be forgiven. He attended parties; he laughed; he touched; he healed; he spent time with tax collectors, sinners, wealthy persons, the poor, and lepers.

"We know these things about Jesus. It is important, though, that we take time to reflect upon how we can live like Jesus. Think about how you spend your time and your talents.

"I would like to give you fifteen minutes to be still and alone to reflect on how you are following Jesus. For some of you this might be difficult. If being quiet is difficult for you, please respect others' needs to take time to be alone.

"In order to help you quiet yourselves, I would like to show you some slides. After the slides, locate a place where you can be still and comfortable. After fifteen minutes, I will make an announcement and invite you to gather in your small-group meeting rooms."

1:30 p.m. Small group 2

Staff: one person for each small group

Purposes: to facilitate a discussion about the retreatants' reflections from the quiet time and to help them plan for the liturgy

Materials needed for each group: index cards and pencils

Description of activities
1. Introduction (5 min.): "As we begin the discussion, I want to remind you of the guidelines we discussed this morning." Remind the retreatants of the importance of cooperation, listening, acceptance, and participation by all.

2. Discussion (20 min.): Encourage all to participate in a discussion, using the questions suggested below.
- How do you use your time? for yourself? for others?
- What are your talents?
- How do you use your talents?
- Is it important for you to follow Jesus? Explain.
- What can you do to act more like Jesus? Be specific.
- What goal could you set for yourself as you leave the retreat?

3. Affirmation (15 min.): Invite the retreatants to go around the circle and speak to each other about characteristics they see and appreciate in each person. Make sure they speak directly to the person they are affirming.

4. Liturgy preparation (15 min.): "There is one last thing that we need to do. Each small group is responsible for some aspect of the eucharistic liturgy. Our group is responsible for _____. Let's use these fifteen minutes to prepare our part for the liturgy." Help the group determine how it will carry out its responsibilities, using index cards and pencils to note specific assignments. Suggested assignments for the small groups follow.
- Group A—Proclaim the first reading (Eph. 5:8–17).
- Group B—Read the response (Ps. 37:3–4,5–6,23–24) with the antiphon "Here I am, Lord; I come to do your will."
- Group C—Offer the Prayer of the Faithful.
- Group D—Present the offertory gifts.
- Group E—Read the Communion meditation, "One Solitary Life," Handout 1–B, and pass out copies of the handout to the retreatants at the conclusion of the liturgy.

5. Closure: End with a closing prayer and invite the retreatants to come to where the liturgy is being celebrated.

2:45 p.m. Liturgy

The small groups carry out those parts of the liturgy for which they are responsible.

3:45 p.m. Concretizing

Staff: one person

Purposes: to remind the retreatants of the retreat theme and to challenge them to keep alive any commitments or resolutions that they have made as a result of the retreat experience

Materials needed: a Bible

Description of activities

"Six hours ago you gathered here to begin your day of retreat. You heard a reading from the prophet Jeremiah. Jeremiah said, 'Lord, I am too young. I don't know what to say.' And the Lord reassured him, 'I will give you the words to say.' You have been challenged during this day to think about your relationship with Jesus. You have discussed your beliefs in small and large groups. You have listened to your peers' beliefs. You spent quiet time by yourself. And you affirmed one another.

"During the first small group, you set a goal for yourself. Have you reached that goal? If you have, you are the person responsible for that. I challenge you to take home and put into practice any new resolutions you set for yourself. Home will be the same when you return. If any change has taken place today, it is within you. Keep it alive. Call upon Jesus frequently to assist you.

"We will continue to pray for you. I encourage you to pray for each other. I would like to close with the words of Jesus."

Read John 15:12–17.

4:00 p.m. Departure

What to Consider Before the Retreat

The introduction to this manual contains useful information about what to consider in advance of a retreat. The reader is here referred to that material, and specific additions for this retreat are also noted below.

Details in advance: See pages 11–12.

Personnel needed: See page 12.

Agenda for the staff preretreat planning meeting: See page 12. When planning the liturgy, consider using the following readings.
- First reading—Eph. 5:8–17
- Responsorial psalm—Ps. 37:3–4,5–6,23–24, with the antiphon "Here I am, Lord; I come to do your will."
- Gospel—Luke 6:12–16
- Communion meditation—"One Solitary Life," Handout 1–B

You may use the "Planning Sheet for Eucharistic Liturgy" on page 107 to prepare for this liturgy.

Materials needed: See page 12. In addition, bring a slide projector, a screen, and appropriate slides of nature or of people helping others.

Attributes of Jesus

HANDOUT 1-A

Directions: Carefully read the list of attributes of Jesus. Think about each one. Choose the five attributes that mean the most to you. Circle the attributes and then rank them in the order of their importance to you by marking from 1 to 5 in the boxes.

- ☐ Jesus as healer
- ☐ Jesus as teacher
- ☐ Jesus as Son of God
- ☐ Jesus as risen one
- ☐ Jesus as lover
- ☐ Jesus as a man for others
- ☐ Jesus as forgiver
- ☐ Jesus as God
- ☐ Jesus as human being
- ☐ Jesus as miracle worker
- ☐ Jesus as friend of sinners
- ☐ Jesus as pray-er
- ☐ Jesus as life-giver
- ☐ Jesus as a man of faith
- ☐ Jesus as God-Man

He was born in an obscure village,
    the child of a peasant woman.
He grew up in still another village,
    where he worked in a carpentry shop until he was thirty.
Then for three years he was an itinerant preacher.

He never wrote a book.
He never held an office.
He never had a family or owned a house.
He didn't go to college.
He never visited a big city.
He never traveled two hundred miles from the place
    where he was born.
He did none of the things one usually associates
    with greatness.
He had no credentials but himself.

He was only thirty-three when the tide of public opinion
    turned against him.
His friends ran away.
He was turned over to his enemies and went through
    the mockery of a trial.
He was nailed to a cross between two thieves.
While he was dying, his executioners gambled for his clothing,
    the only property he had on earth.
When he was dead, he was laid in a borrowed grave,
    through the pity of a friend.

Nineteen centuries have come and gone,
    and today he is the central figure of the human race,
    and the leader of humankind's progress.
All the armies that ever marched,
    all the navies that ever sailed,
    all the parliaments that ever sat,
    all the kings that ever reigned, put together . . .
    have not affected the life of people on this earth as much as that . . .
    One Solitary Life.

Retreat 2
Confirmation

Goals

The retreat "Confirmation" is designed for high school students who are preparing to be confirmed. It is a single-day program for twenty to forty retreatants.

The goals of the retreat are the following:
1. The retreatants will share their beliefs and questions about the Sacrament of Confirmation.
2. The retreatants will examine the meaning of the Profession of Faith.
3. The retreatants will renew their baptismal commitment.

Schedule

9:00 a.m.	Arrival
9:30 a.m.	Introduction and prayer
10:15 a.m.	Small group 1
11:30 a.m.	Lunch
12:30 p.m.	The Profession of Faith — input
12:50 p.m.	Quiet time
1:30 p.m.	Small group 2
2:30 p.m.	Break
2:45 p.m.	Liturgy
3:45 p.m.	Concretizing
4:00 p.m.	Departure

Retreat Activities

9:00 a.m. Arrival

Two staff members welcome and register the retreatants and have them fill out name tags.

9:30 a.m. Introduction and prayer

Staff: two people (including one to assist with the handouts and the tape recorder)

Purposes: to lead the retreat community in prayer, to introduce the theme of the retreat, to introduce the retreat staff, and to explain guidelines for using the retreat facility

Materials needed: a Bible; Handout 2-A, "Holy Spirit Prayer"; a tape recorder; and an appropriate tape

Description of activities

Part 1: "Welcome to your retreat. My name is _____. As we begin this day, I invite you to take a moment to quietly call upon the Spirit of Jesus to guide you today." Pause.

"During the past few months, you have been preparing to confirm your faith. As you know, the Sacrament of Confirmation is one of the sacraments of initiation. In Baptism, you are born again. You are nourished in the Eucharist. In Confirmation you are strengthened by the Spirit of Jesus. Please listen to this passage from Scripture. I think it speaks directly to you today. Try to imagine yourself in the room with the other Apostles. Be aware of how you feel when Jesus speaks these words to you." Slowly, read John 20:19–21.

"When you confirm your faith, you will take on the responsibility to be a witness of Jesus in both word and action. You will also be more closely bound to the People of God. Becoming a part of the missionary activity of the Church is quite a responsibility. It is because of the importance of this step in your life that we have a day of retreat planned for you. I invite you to examine your own feelings, beliefs, and concerns about the Sacrament of Confirmation.

"The schedule is quite full. There will be two times when you will meet in small discussion groups. This afternoon you will have some quiet time by yourself. We will close the day with a renewal of our baptismal promises and the celebration of the eucharistic liturgy.

"In order for you to get the most out of this retreat experience, I encourage you to leave behind any stereotypes you may have. Give others a chance to show who they truly are. Try to trust yourself, other retreatants, the staff, and the program. Perhaps the most important encouragement I offer you is to take responsibility for fully participating in each activity. You are the person responsible for what you get out of this day.

"Before I introduce the staff to you, let's join together in prayer, asking the Spirit of God to renew us. [Distribute Handout 2–A.] Please read aloud the 'Holy Spirit Prayer.'" Lead the retreatants in reading the prayer.

Part 2: See part 2 of the "Description of activities" on page 14 of Retreat 1 for the introductions and the practical details. At the conclusion, invite the retreatants to the location of the next activity.

10:15 a.m. Small group 1

Staff: one person for each small group

Purposes: to assist the retreatants in establishing small-group discussion rules, to encourage the retreatants to set a personal goal for the retreat, to facilitate the discussion, and to help the retreatants plan for the liturgy

Materials needed for each group: an index card and a pencil for each retreatant, a roll of masking tape, two large pieces of butcher paper, and a felt-tip marker

Description of activities

1. Introduction (10 min.): "How is everybody doing? [Pause.] Let's begin with some simple introductions. As we go around the circle, please tell us your name and something unique about you. After each person introduces himself or herself, feel free to ask questions or comment on anything the person said." Have each person introduce himself or herself and encourage others to respond in some way.

2. Guidelines (5 min.): "As you were told during the introductory meeting, this retreat is meant to be a time for you to think about your own beliefs. You have been taught a lot over the years. We think it is important for you to have some time to get away and think about what all of this means to you. Since we will be discussing our beliefs and experiences with one another, we need to set some guidelines for discussion. I will write them down and hang the paper on the wall so we can easily refer to the guidelines, if needed. In your experience, what have you found to be helpful in a small-group discussion?"

With the felt-tip marker, write on the butcher paper the rules named. Make sure the following are included: confidentiality, respect, no put-downs, honesty, and an attempt to participate by all.

3. Personal goals (5 min.): "Take a moment to think about what you hope to get out of this retreat. Time will go quickly today. It is because of this that I ask you to set a goal for yourself for this day of retreat. I will give each of you a pencil and an index card to write down that goal." Pass out the pencils and the index cards.

4. Discussion (45 min.): Encourage the retreatants to participate in a discussion of the questions suggested below. If the group is reluctant to discuss, pair each retreatant with another person for a two-minute dyad on one of the questions. Then return to the group discussion. If the discussion moves in another direction than planned, be flexible. The retreatants might need to talk about other issues. Remember, they need a safe place to explore their questions. Above all, make sure the ground rules are observed.

- Why did you join this retreat?
- How do you feel about being here?
- Do you have any hopes or fears for this day?
- What does it mean for you to confirm your faith?
- Whose faith are you confirming? Yours? Your parents'? Your teachers'?
- Will you act any differently after you are confirmed? If yes, how?
- What has been helpful for you in the instruction class?
- What has been difficult for you in the instruction class?
- If you were in charge of the Confirmation class, what would you add to the preparation?

5. Summary (5 min.): "Thank you for trusting one another. I encourage you to continue to explore your feelings, beliefs, and experiences. I believe it is very important and healthy for growth. Quite often it clarifies a direction for the future. Before we close, does anyone have any comments for the group?" Go around the circle, giving everyone a chance to speak.

6. Liturgy preparation (5 min.): "There is one last thing that we need to do. Each small group is responsible for some aspect of the eucharistic liturgy. Our group is responsible for _____. At lunchtime we need to take care of the preparations for our part." Suggested assignments for the small groups follow.
- Group A—Introduce the first reading (Ezek. 36:24–28).
- Group B—Proclaim the first reading (Ezek. 36:24–28).
- Group C—Read the response (Ps. 104:1,24,27–28, 30–31,33–34) with the antiphon "Lord, send out your Spirit, and renew the face of the earth."
- Group D—Offer the Prayer of the Faithful.
- Group E—Present the offertory gifts.

7. Closure: End with a closing prayer and explain the schedule for the afternoon.

11:30 a.m. Lunch

One staff person is available to make announcements and to choose a retreatant to lead the group in prayer before the meal.

12:30 p.m. The Profession of Faith—input

Staff: two people (including one to assist with distributing handouts and pencils)

Purposes: to present the four basic beliefs listed in the Profession of Faith and to introduce the value of quiet time

Materials needed: Handout 2–B, "Quiet-Time Questions on the Profession of Faith"; an 8½-by-11-inch piece of paper and a pencil for each retreatant

Description of activities

"This afternoon I invite you to take time to reflect upon your beliefs as a Christian. This activity is divided into two parts. First of all, I will briefly remind you of our Profession of Faith. After that I will give you some quiet time to be alone to reflect. When the quiet time ends, we will go directly to our small groups. These will be the same as this morning.

"As I examine our creed, I find that it is divided into four main beliefs. This simplifies things for me to look at it in this way. See what you think.

"Belief no. 1—I believe in God. We then explain various ways that we experience God. We know God as the Father, as the Creator, as the Son and our Brother in Jesus, and as the Holy Spirit. The Profession of Faith goes into more detail than this, though. That is because when it was drawn up, certain groups were claiming other beliefs. And the Church had to make sure we were clear on our understanding. The main idea seems simply to be that we believe in God.

"Belief no. 2—I believe in the People of God. We express this when we talk about the Church and the communion of saints. The saints are the People of God who have gone before us.

"Belief no. 3—I believe in the forgiveness of sins. This is the one *action* in which we profess to believe. Forgiveness is the center of our faith and our relationship with God and one another. How I wish we could live that. Imagine how much personal healing would take place if we could just forgive ourselves. Imagine how much relational healing would take place if we could forgive one another! And yet that is what we are professing to believe. The challenge here is for our actions to match our words.

"Belief no. 4—I believe in life. We believe in the gift of life now and in life everlasting.

"At Mass each Sunday, together as a faith community, we profess our beliefs. Soon you will confirm your faith. What does this mean to you in light of your Profession of Faith? During the next half hour I invite you to reflect upon the meaning of your Confirmation. Each of you will be given a handout with some questions, a blank piece of paper, and a pencil. Write down any reflections or questions you may have."

Explain the areas set aside for this activity. Be specific about the locations. If the retreatants are allowed to go outside, be sure some adults are present to supervise so that talkative retreatants do not disturb those wishing to use the quiet time. Hand out the "Quiet-Time Questions on the Profession of Faith" (Handout 2–B) and pencils, and invite the retreatants to go to one of the quiet areas.

12:50 p.m. Quiet time

Staff: two people to supervise the retreatants

1:30 p.m. Small group 2

Staff: one person for each small group

Purpose: to facilitate a discussion of the retreatants' reflections from the quiet time

Materials needed: none

Description of activities

1. Introduction: "As we begin the discussion, I want to remind you of the guidelines we established this morning. [Allow time for the retreatants to read the guidelines posted on the wall.] Does anyone feel that we need to add or revise any guidelines?"

2. Discussion of questions: "This discussion time is meant to give you a chance to talk with one another about thoughts you had during the quiet time. Please refer to your papers. Is there any particular question that you want to discuss or hear others address?"

Facilitate the discussion, referring to the "Quiet-Time Questions on the Profession of Faith" handout. Again, make sure the ground rules are observed. Try to encourage everyone to participate to some degree. Be sure to allow time for the last question to be discussed.

3. Closure: Invite each retreatant to offer a closing statement. Remind the group of their responsibilities for the liturgy. Close with a short prayer.

2:30 p.m. Break

2:45 p.m. Liturgy

The small groups carry out those parts of the liturgy for which they are responsible.

During the penitential rite or after the homily, invite the retreatants to renew their baptismal commitment. Remind them that at each Easter Vigil Mass we do this as a faith community.

Renewal of baptismal commitment
- Do you reject Satan and all his works and all his empty promises? We do.
- Do you believe in God, the Father almighty, creator of heaven and earth? We do.
- Do you believe in Jesus Christ, his only Son, our Lord, who was born of the Virgin Mary, was crucified, died, and was buried, rose from the dead, and is now seated at the right hand of the Father? We do.
- Do you believe in the Holy Spirit, the holy catholic Church, the communion of saints, the forgiveness of sins, the resurrection of the body, and life everlasting? We do.

3:45 p.m. Concretizing

Staff: one person

Purposes: to remind the retreatants of the retreat theme and to challenge them to keep alive any commitments or resolutions that they have made as a result of the retreat experience

Materials needed: a Bible

Description of activities
"Six hours ago you gathered here to begin your day of retreat. I invite you to take time to review the day. During the first small group you set a goal for yourself. How have you done on that goal? What do you still need to do? Is there a goal you could set for yourself as you leave the retreat?

"This afternoon you took some quiet time to reflect upon your beliefs. Whose faith are you confirming? What does it mean to you to witness to Jesus in word and action? Will people know Jesus is your Lord by the way you treat them?

"I challenge you to take home with you and put into practice any new resolutions you set for yourself. Home will be the same when you return. If any change has taken place today, it is within you. Keep it alive. Let the Spirit of Jesus strengthen you to live a life worthy of your call. We will continue to pray for you. Please do the same for one another. Remember that you are the first generation of a new Church. The Second Vatican Council ended shortly before you were born. The Church is in a time of renewal. I challenge you to take your place in that renewal as the Spirit of Jesus guides you.

"I would like to close with the reading from John's Gospel that we heard as we began this day. Please try again to hear this message as the one spoken to you by Jesus today." Read John 20:19–21.

4:00 p.m. Departure

What to Consider Before the Retreat

The introduction to this manual contains useful information about what to consider in advance of a retreat. The reader is here referred to that material, and specific additions for this retreat are also noted below.

Details in advance: See pages 11–12.

Personnel needed: See page 12.

Agenda for the staff preretreat planning meeting: See page 12. When planning the liturgy, consider using the following readings.
- First reading—Ezek. 36:24–28
- Responsorial psalm—Ps. 104:1,24,27–28,30–31, 33–34, with the antiphon "Lord, send out your Spirit, and renew the face of the earth."
- Gospel—John 14:23–26

You may use the "Planning Sheet for Eucharistic Liturgy" on page 107 to prepare for this liturgy.

Materials needed: See page 12. In addition, the handouts that follow should be reproduced in advance, with each handout on its own page.

Come, Holy Spirit, fill the hearts of your faithful
and enkindle in them the fire of your love.
Send forth your Spirit and they shall be created,
and you shall renew the face of the earth.

Directions: Read and reflect upon the Profession of Faith and the questions below. Write down your thoughts or questions on the paper provided.

We believe in one God,

> the Father, the Almighty, maker of heaven and earth, of all that is seen and unseen.

> We believe in one Lord, Jesus Christ, the only Son of God, eternally begotten of the Father, God from God, Light from Light, true God from true God, begotten, not made, one in Being with the Father. Through him all things were made. For us and for our salvation he came down from heaven: by the power of the Holy Spirit he was born of the Virgin Mary, and became man. For our sake he was crucified under Pontius Pilate; he suffered, died, and was buried. On the third day he rose again in fulfillment of the Scriptures; he ascended into heaven and is seated at the right hand of the Father. He will come again in glory to judge the living and the dead, and his kingdom will have no end.

> We believe in the Holy Spirit, the Lord, the giver of life, who proceeds from the Father and the Son. With the Father and the Son he is worshiped and glorified. He has spoken through the Prophets.

We believe in one holy catholic and apostolic Church.

We acknowledge one baptism for the forgiveness of sins.

We look for the resurrection of the dead, and the life of the world to come. Amen.

1. What do you believe about God?
2. What do you believe about the People of God?
3. What do you believe about forgiveness?
4. What do you believe about life?
5. What does it mean to you to be a follower of Jesus?
6. What is the message of Jesus as you understand it?
7. What draws you to the message of Jesus?
8. If Jesus were to walk the earth today, do you think he would be happy with his Church? Explain.
9. How are you able to witness for Jesus in your words and actions? Be specific.

Retreat 3
Vocation

Goals

The retreat "Vocation" is designed for high school-aged participants. It is a single-day program for twenty to forty retreatants.

The goals of the retreat are the following:

1. The retreatants will discuss vocation as their call to be People of God.
2. The retreatants will examine their personal skills, talents, hopes, and dreams.
3. The retreatants will discuss various lifestyles within the Christian tradition.

Schedule

9:00 a.m.	Arrival
9:15 a.m.	Introduction and prayer
9:45 a.m.	Small group 1
11:00 a.m.	Break
11:15 a.m.	Quiet time
12:00 m.	Lunch
12:45 p.m.	Small group 2
2:15 p.m.	Break
2:30 p.m.	Liturgy
3:15 p.m.	Concretizing
3:30 p.m.	Departure

Retreat Activities

9:00 a.m. Arrival

Two staff members welcome and register the retreatants and have them fill out name tags.

9:15 a.m. Introduction and prayer

Staff: two people (including one to assist with the handouts and the tape recorder)

Purposes: to lead the retreat community in prayer, to introduce the theme of the retreat, to introduce the retreat staff, and to explain guidelines for using the retreat facility

Materials needed: a Bible; Handout 3–A, "Vocation Prayer"; a tape recorder; and an appropriate tape (e.g., "Searchin' So Long" by Chicago)

Description of activities

Part 1: "Welcome to your retreat. My name is _____. As we begin this day, I invite you to take a moment to quietly call upon our loving God to speak to you today." Pause.

"Did you ever want to be a saint? Perhaps you once thought about being a saint but quickly dismissed the idea because it seemed to be too hard or just plain impossible. Well, whether you have thought about it before or not, today I encourage you to spend some time thinking about that question. Do you want to be a saint?

"A saint is someone who makes an earnest effort to follow Jesus by loving God and trying to love others as Jesus did. In the eyes of the Church there are many requirements before a person is recognized officially as a saint. However, in God's eyes it is really much easier.

"Being a saint fits right into the theme of today's retreat. Our theme is vocation. I believe the vocation or call by God for each of us is to love as Jesus did. Our personal vocation is lived out in a particular lifestyle and by doing a particular type of work. Sometimes a person's vocation is understood to be that of a priest or sister. A priest or sister chooses a particular lifestyle and a particular type of work. A single person and a married person have vocations also.

"In the early 1970s, the musical group Chicago came out with a song entitled '(I've Been) Searchin' So Long.' The lyrics speak of finding meaning in life. I would like to play the song for you. Listen to see if the words capture a feeling that you have had. Does your life have meaning?" Play the song.

"I hope that you will have a sense of peace and trust when you leave today. Perhaps the song captures that feeling. The schedule for today is full. There will be time for you to be alone to quietly reflect upon your personal call. Two times we will meet in small discussion groups. As a sign of our call to be the People of God, we will close the day by celebrating the eucharistic liturgy.

"In order for you to get the most out of the retreat, I encourage you to leave behind any stereotypes you may have of anyone here. Trust yourself, other retreatants, the staff, and the program. Take the responsibility upon yourself for fully participating in each activity. You are the person who is ultimately responsible for what you get out of the day. We will be praying for you. I also encourage you to pray for each other.

"Before I introduce the rest of the staff to you, let's join together in prayer, asking our loving God to help us to know our call. [Distribute Handout 3–A.] Please join in praying the 'Vocation Prayer.' " Lead the retreatants in reading the prayer.

Part 2: See part 2 of the "Description of activities" on page 14 of Retreat 1 for the introductions and the practical details. At the conclusion, invite the retreatants to the location of the next activity.

9:45 a.m. Small group 1

Staff: one person for each small group

Purposes: to assist the retreatants in establishing small-group discussion rules, to encourage the retreatants to set a personal goal for the retreat, to facilitate a discussion about lifestyles and vocations, and to help the retreatants plan for the liturgy

Materials needed for each group: an index card and a pencil for each retreatant, a roll of masking tape, two large pieces of butcher paper, and a felt-tip marker

Description of activities

1. Introduction (10 min.): "I would like to begin with simple introductions. We will go around the circle. As you introduce yourself, please tell us your name and why you chose to come on this retreat. After a person has been introduced, please feel free to respond to him or her, or ask that person questions you might have regarding his or her introductory comments." Proceed with introductions. Encourage the retreatants to talk freely about their reasons for attending the retreat.

2. Guidelines (5 min.): "During this retreat we will meet as a small group two times. These discussions are meant to give you a chance to articulate your questions and ideas as well as to expose you to the thinking of others. Before we do begin the discussion, I would like for you to establish some guidelines for discussion. What adds to a good discussion? I will write down the guidelines you decide upon. I will hang them on the wall so we can refer to them if necessary."

With the felt-tip marker, write the guidelines on the butcher paper. Make sure the following are included: confidentiality, respect, no put-downs, honesty, and an attempt to participate by all.

3. Personal goals (5 min.): "When you introduced yourself, you spoke briefly about your reason for coming on the retreat. Could you set a goal for yourself for the day? I would like you to write something down and then refer to this throughout the day. The time goes quickly, and it is easy to lose the focus." Pass out the pencils and the index cards.

4. Discussion (45 minutes): Encourage all to participate in the discussion of the questions suggested below. If the group is slow to discuss, pair each retreatant with another person for a two-minute dyad. Then return to the group discussion. Make sure the ground rules are observed. Be flexible. If the discussion seems to move in an unexpected direction, be open to the needs of the retreatants.
- What is your image of a saint?
- Have you ever thought about being a saint?
- What lifestyle is attractive to you?
- What are the joys and hardships of this lifestyle?
- Who do you know who lives this same lifestyle? How do you view him or her?
- What profession is attractive to you?
- What are the joys and hardships of this profession?
- Who do you know who works in this profession? How do you view him or her?

5. Summary (5 minutes): "Thank you for trusting one another. I encourage you to continue to explore and talk about these issues with one another. Hearing other ideas can expand our own limited perspectives. Before we close the discussion, does anyone have a closing comment to make to the group?" Go around the circle giving everyone a chance to make a closing comment.

6. Liturgy preparation (5 min.): "There is one last thing that we need to do before we take a break. Each small group is responsible for some aspect of the eucharistic liturgy. Our group is responsible for _____. At lunch we need to take care of the preparations for our part." Suggested assignments for the small groups follow.
- Group A—Introduce the first reading (Eph. 4:1–6).
- Group B—Proclaim the first reading (Eph. 4:1–6).
- Group C—Read the response (Ps. 40:5–6,9–10,17) with the antiphon "Here I am, Lord; I come to do your will."
- Group D—Offer the Prayer of the Faithful.
- Group E—Present the offertory gifts.

7. Closure: End with a closing prayer and explain the schedule for the afternoon.

11:00 a.m. Break

11:15 a.m. Quiet time

Staff: two people (including one to assist with distributing materials and supervising quiet time)

Purpose: to introduce the value of reflection through quiet time spent alone

Materials needed: Handout 3–B, "Quiet-Time Questions on Vocation," and pencils

Description of activities

"Within your small groups you had time to discuss certain lifestyles and professions that are attractive to you. For most of you, your choices are influenced by your individual skills, talents, hopes, and dreams. As men and women of God, we need to develop our talents and dream our dreams. I believe that God speaks to us individually through our unique life circumstances. In order to hear God speak to us, though, we need to make ourselves available to listen.

"During the next thirty minutes, I invite you to spend time alone in order to pray and reflect. Listen to God speak to you through Scripture, your thoughts, feelings, and urges. Trust that you are really able to understand God's call. Scripture says, 'Nothing is impossible with God.'

"Each of you will be given a paper with a scriptural passage and some questions. After you find a quiet place to be alone, read the passage and imagine that Jesus is right there talking to you. Read the questions. Perhaps other questions will come to mind; write down your reflections. This is your time to listen. If it is difficult for you to sit quietly, please respect others in their attempts to spend this time alone."

Explain the areas available to be used during this activity. Be specific. Be sure an adult is present to supervise. Give out the "Quiet-Time Questions on Vocation" (Handout 3–B) and pencils. Invite the retreatants to begin the activity.

12:00 m. Lunch

One staff person is available to make announcements and to choose a retreatant to lead the group in grace before the meal.

12:45 p.m. Small group 2

Staff: one person for each small group

Purpose: to facilitate a discussion about the retreatants' skills, talents, and dreams

Materials needed: an 8½-by-11-inch piece of paper and a pencil for each retreatant

Description of activities

1. Introduction (15 min.): "How is everyone doing so far? How did the quiet time go for you? [Give adequate time for the group members to talk about their experiences.] This small-group session is a time to explore your skills and talents and to talk about your hopes and dreams. As we begin the discussion, I want to remind you of the guidelines for discussion we established this morning." Allow time for the retreatants to read the guidelines posted on the wall.

2. Reflection (10 min.): Pass to each retreatant a pencil and a piece of 8½-by-11-inch paper. "In order to know our calling, we need to be aware of our God-given talents and skills. Think a moment about your unique skills and

talents. Make a list of as many as you can. If you have a difficult time thinking of these, we will help you." Allow time for everyone to make a list. Then divide the group into pairs.

3. Activity (15 min.): "Each of you has a partner. I would like you to spend some time with your partner, telling that person about your unique talents and skills. Then explain to your partner how these talents or skills could be used as you live out your call from God—or ask your partner to help you understand how they could be used, if you're not sure." Allow five to seven minutes, and then have the retreatants choose a new partner. Do the activity a second and a third time. Each person should meet with at least three others.

4. Discussion (25 min.): "I would like to give everyone a chance to talk with the group about any insights you have gained by talking with your partners.

"Are there any hopes or dreams that you have for the future? Remember, soon you will be the leaders of our society. What would you like to see take place within the next twenty years for you personally and for the world? Is there anything you can do to help this happen?

"During quiet time you thought about how you might arrange your daily schedule in order to strengthen your relationship with God. Can you give some specifics?

"What do you need to leave behind in your life in order to follow Jesus?"

Encourage the retreatants to participate. Remind the retreatants of the guidelines, if necessary.

5. Closure (15 min.): Invite each retreatant to offer a closing statement to the group. Remind the group of their responsibilities for the liturgy. Ask a retreatant to close the discussion with a prayer.

2:15 p.m. Break

2:30 p.m. Liturgy

The small groups carry out those parts of the liturgy for which they are responsible.

During the closing of the liturgy, invite the retreatants to bow their heads for a vocation blessing such as the one suggested below.

Closing blessing

May God enrich you with the gifts of faith, hope, and love, so that what you do in this life will bring you to the happiness of everlasting life. [Response: Amen.]

May God direct your steps and show you how to walk in loving ways. [Response: Amen.]

May God enlighten you to know what is right and good until you enter your heavenly inheritance. [Response: Amen.]

May almighty God bless you, the Father and the Son and the Holy Spirit. [Response: Amen.]

3:15 p.m. Concretizing

Staff: one person

Purposes: to remind the retreatants of the retreat theme and to challenge the retreatants to keep alive any commitments or resolutions that they have made as a result of the retreat experience

Materials needed: a Bible

Description of activities

"Six hours ago you gathered here to begin your day of retreat. I invite you to take time to review the day. During the first small group, you set a goal for yourself. How have you done on that goal? What do you still need to do? Is there a goal you could set for yourself as you leave the retreat?

"This afternoon you took some quiet time to reflect upon your hopes and dreams for the future. Are you willing to try to be a saint as you live out your chosen lifestyle and profession? Will others know that Jesus is your Lord by the way you treat them?

"I challenge you to take home with you and put into practice any new resolutions you set for yourself. Home will be the same when you return. If any change has taken place today, it is within you. Keep it alive. Let the Spirit of Jesus strengthen you to live a life worthy of your call. We will continue to pray for you. Please do the same for one another. Remember you are the first generation of a new Church. The Second Vatican Council ended shortly before you were born. The Church is in a time of renewal. I challenge you to take your place in that renewal as the Spirit of Jesus guides you.

"I would like to close with a reading from John's Gospel. Please try to hear this message as the one spoken to you by Jesus today." Read John 15:12–17.

3:30 p.m. Departure

What to Consider Before the Retreat

The introduction to this manual contains useful information about what to consider in advance of a retreat. The reader is here referred to that material, and specific additions for this retreat are also noted below.

Details in advance: See pages 11–12.

Personnel needed: See page 12.

Agenda for the staff preretreat planning meeting: See page 12. When planning the liturgy, consider using the following readings.
• First reading—Eph. 4:1–6
• Responsorial psalm—Ps. 40:5–6,9–10,17, with the antiphon "Here I am, Lord; I come to do your will."
• Gospel—Matt. 9:35–38

You may use the "Planning Sheet for Eucharistic Liturgy" on page 107 to prepare for this liturgy.

Materials needed: See page 12. In addition, the handouts that follow should be reproduced in advance, with each handout on its own page.

Vocation Prayer

Loving God,
Help me to know clearly the work that you are calling me to in my life.
Walk with me and strengthen me with your grace
    so that I might answer your call.
Grant me charity, love, generosity,
    and a lasting dedication to do your will.
I offer this prayer in Jesus' name.
Amen.

Quiet-Time Questions on Vocation

Directions: Prayerfully read and reflect upon the following scriptural passage and questions. Write down your reflections.

> **As Jesus was walking along the Sea of Galilee he watched two brothers, Simon now known as Peter, and his brother Andrew, casting a net into the sea. They were fishermen. He said to them, "Come after me and I will make you fishers of men." They immediately abandoned their nets and became his followers. He walked along farther and caught sight of two other brothers, James, Zebedee's son, and his brother John. They too were in their boat, getting their nets in order with their father, Zebedee. He called them, and immediately they abandoned boat and father to follow him. (Matthew 4:18–22, NAB)**

- What do you need to leave behind in your life in order to follow Jesus? (laziness, selfishness, jealousy, greed, revenge?)

- What do you need to do in order to strengthen your relationship with God? (pray, study your faith, reconcile relationships?)

- How could you arrange your daily schedule in order to strengthen your relationship with God?

- Have you ever thought of making a commitment as a priest, a brother, or a sister?

- Have you ever thought of remaining single?

- Have you ever thought of raising a family?

- What are your hopes and dreams for the future?

Retreat 4
Christian Conscience Formation

Goals

The retreat "Christian Conscience Formation" is designed for older (tenth-, eleventh-, and twelfth-grade) retreatants.

The goals of the retreat are the following:
1. The retreatants will explore scriptural passages regarding conscience.
2. The retreatants will understand what constitutes an informed conscience.
3. The retreatants will learn basic problem-solving skills.

Schedule

9:00 a.m.	Arrival
9:15 a.m.	Introduction and prayer
9:45 a.m.	Small group 1
10:45 a.m.	Break
11:00 a.m.	Scriptural search
12:00 m.	Lunch
1:00 p.m.	Small group 2
2:15 p.m.	Break
2:30 p.m.	Liturgy
3:15 p.m.	Concretizing
3:30 p.m.	Departure

Retreat Activities

9:00 a.m. Arrival

Two staff members welcome and register the retreatants and have them fill out name tags.

9:15 a.m. Introduction and prayer

Staff: two people (including one to assist with the handouts)

Purposes: to lead the retreat community in prayer, to introduce the theme of the retreat, to introduce the retreat staff, and to explain guidelines for using the retreat facility

Materials needed: a Bible and Handout 4–A, "Conscience Prayer"

Description of activities

Part 1: "Welcome to your retreat. My name is _____. As we begin this day, I invite you to offer a silent prayer asking for God's guidance." Pause.

"The theme for today's retreat is 'Christian Conscience Formation.' Within our society, a variety of attitudes, actions, and lifestyles are acceptable. Some actions that were forbidden by civil law in the past are now legal. There is a tremendous amount of peer pressure pushing you to go beyond your limits. How do you decide what is right and wrong? Do you have any guidelines to use when you are confronted with a moral choice? How do you form and nurture your own conscience?

"During this retreat, you will have the opportunity to reflect upon these questions. You will be invited to examine scriptural passages that refer to conscience, to discuss what constitutes an informed conscience, and to learn some basic problem-solving skills. As a sign of our unity, we will close the day by celebrating the eucharistic liturgy.

"In order for you to get the most out of the retreat, I encourage you to trust yourself, the other retreatants, the staff, and the program. Take the responsibility upon yourself to fully participate in each activity. You are the person who is ultimately responsible for what you get out of the day. The staff will be praying for you. I encourage you to pray for one another."

Distribute Handout 4–A. "Before I introduce the rest of the staff to you, please join me in praying the 'Conscience Prayer.' " Lead the retreatants in reading the prayer.

Part 2: See part 2 of the "Description of activities" on page 14 of Retreat 1 for the introductions and the practical details. At the conclusion, invite the retreatants to the location of the next activity.

9:45 a.m. Small group 1

Staff: one person for each small group

Purposes: to assist the retreatants in establishing small-group discussion rules, to encourage the retreatants to set a personal goal for the retreat, to facilitate a discussion about conscience, and to help the retreatants plan for the liturgy

Materials needed for each group: an index card and a pencil for each retreatant, a roll of masking tape, two large pieces of butcher paper, and a felt-tip marker

Description of activities

1. Introduction (10 min.): "Let's begin with some simple introductions. As we go around the circle, please tell us your name and the reason why you decided to attend this retreat." Have each person introduce himself or herself and encourage others to respond in some way.

2. Guidelines (5 min.): "During this retreat we will meet as a small group two times. These discussions are meant to give you a chance to articulate your questions and ideas as well as to expose you to the thinking of others. Before we do begin the discussion, I would like you to establish some guidelines for discussion. What adds to a good discussion? I will write down the guidelines as you decide upon them. I will then hang them on the wall so we can refer to them if necessary."

With the felt-tip marker, write the rules on the butcher paper. Make sure the following are included: confidentiality, respect, no put-downs, honesty, and an attempt to participate by all.

3. Personal goals (5 min.): "When you introduced yourself, you spoke briefly about your reason for coming on the retreat. Could you set a goal for yourself for the day? I would like you to write down a goal and then refer to it throughout the day. The time goes quickly, and it is easy to lose the focus." Pass out the pencils and the index cards.

4. Discussion (30 min.): Encourage all to participate in the discussion of the questions suggested below. Make sure the ground rules are observed. Record the definitions of conscience on the butcher paper.

- How would you define conscience?
- How do you decide what is *right* or *wrong?*
- How has your conscience been formed? Who influenced you? How?
- When was the last time you were confronted with a moral choice? What did you do?
- What guidelines do you use when you are confronted with a moral choice?

5. Summary (5 min.): "Thank you for trusting one another. I encourage you to continue to explore and talk about these issues with one another. Hearing other ideas can expand our own perspective. Before we close the discussion, does anyone have a closing comment to make to the group?" Go around the circle, giving everyone a chance to make a closing comment.

6. Liturgy preparation (5 min.): "There is one last thing that we need to do before we take a break. Each small group is responsible for some aspect of the eucharistic liturgy. Our group is responsible for _____. At lunch we need to take care of the preparations for our part." Suggested assignments for the small groups follow.

- Group A—Introduce the first reading (1 Cor. 10: 23–24,31 – 11:1).

- Group B—Proclaim the first reading (1 Cor. 10: 23–24,31 – 11:1).
- Group C—Read the response (Ps. 26:4–5,6–7,8–9, 11–12) with the antiphon "Your ways, O Lord, make known to me; teach me your paths."
- Group D—Offer the Prayer of the Faithful.
- Group E—Present the offertory gifts

7. Closure: End with a closing prayer and explain the schedule for the rest of the day.

10:45 a.m. Break

11:00 a.m. Scriptural search

Staff: two people (including one to assist with distributing the Bibles and the handouts and supervising the activity)

Purpose: to reflect on passages from Scripture and to share insights about them

Materials needed: a Bible and a pencil for each retreatant; Handout 4–B, "Looking into the Heart: A Scriptural Search"

Description of activities

"During your small groups you defined conscience and talked about the guidelines you use when making moral decisions. You probably found that conscience is not easy to define. Some say it is the person's heart. Others say it is what challenges the heart. Some say it is a feeling. Yet, there are times when feelings are not dependable.

"Whatever the definition, all consciences need to be educated, formed, guided, and directed. I need to find and respect the truth. In the end, I am accountable to the truth. How do I educate my conscience? Cardinal John Henry Newman said that I must go along with my own conscience only after thinking seriously, praying, and seeking every means available of arriving at a right judgment on an issue.

"I believe that the Church is a positive and important teacher of moral values. As a Roman Catholic, I believe that the Holy Spirit guides the People of God. I am not always aware of the truth and sometimes need guidance. So, at times I look to the Church for guidance.

"Studying Scripture and personal prayer are other ways to form my conscience. I believe the truth is within each of us. We need to take time to search for it. I invite you to spend the next thirty minutes prayerfully examining some scriptural passages referring to conscience. In the Jewish Scriptures, the idea of conscience was conveyed by the word *heart.* After thirty minutes we will return and share our reflections with another person.

"Please take a Bible, the handout "Looking into the Heart: A Scriptural Search," and a pencil. Find a quiet place where you are alone. Prayerfully read the scriptural passages listed. Write down any reflections or insights you may have. Does anyone have any questions?"

Give out the Bibles, Handout 4–B, and the pencils. Be sure an adult is present to supervise. After thirty minutes, make an announcement for all to gather together again. Invite the retreatants to turn to another person to share their insights or reflections. Close with instructions for lunch and a brief prayer.

12:00 m. Lunch

One staff person is available to make announcements and to choose a retreatant to lead the group in prayer before the meal.

1:00 p.m. Small group 2

Staff: one person for each small group

Purposes: to assist the retreatants in understanding basic problem solving and to facilitate a discussion of how they would solve some practical problems

Materials needed for each group: an 8½-by-11-inch piece of paper and a pencil for each retreatant, a large piece of butcher paper, and a felt-tip marker

Description of activities

1. Introduction (10 min.): "How are you doing? How was the scriptural search activity for you? Do you have any insights you could share with the group?" Encourage all to respond in some way.

2. Activity (15 min.): "During the first small group we talked about the guidelines you use when confronted with a moral choice. During this meeting, we will look at steps that can be used for solving a particular problem. I would like to present some situations. Each has a particular problem that needs to be addressed. Think about the way you would approach the problem and what steps you would use to solve it. Write down on the paper any ideas you have."

Hand out the pencils and the paper. Read the following situations, one at a time. Allow enough time between each situation for the retreatants to reflect and to write the steps they would use to solve the problem.

- Your sister is sixteen years old. She confides in you that she thinks she is pregnant. What will you do?
- You witness a popular senior selling drugs to your freshman brother. What will you do?
- You convince your parents that you can be trusted. They leave you at home while they go out of town for a weekend. Your friends are looking for a place to party on Saturday night. What will you do?

3. Discussion (40 min.): Addressing one situation at a time, invite the retreatants to talk about the approaches or the steps they wrote for each situation. Ask them to note any patterns in the way they would handle all the

situations. After the three situations have been discussed, write on the butcher paper the "Steps for Problem Solving," have the retreatants copy them on their papers, and discuss the steps. Ask the retreatants to talk about what they would do differently in each situation, using these steps. If there is adequate time, invite the retreatants to suggest another problem situation for the group to work on, using the steps for problem solving. Throughout the discussion, encourage all to participate. Remind them of the guidelines if necessary.

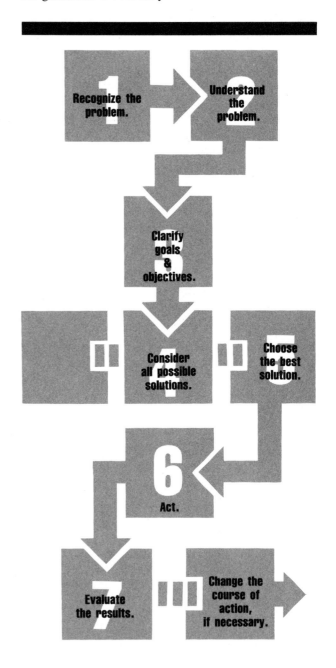

Steps for Problem Solving

4. Closure (10 min.): Invite each retreatant to offer a closing statement to the group. Remind the group of their responsibilities for the liturgy. Ask a retreatant to lead the group in a closing prayer.

2:15 p.m. Break

2:30 p.m. Liturgy

The small groups carry out those parts of the liturgy for which they are responsible.

3:15 p.m. Concretizing

Staff: one person

Purposes: to remind the retreatants of the retreat theme and to challenge them to keep alive any commitments or resolutions that they have made as a result of the retreat experience

Materials needed: none

Description of activities

"Six hours ago we gathered in prayer to begin the retreat. During the day you had time to prayerfully reflect upon Scripture as well as to discuss problem-solving techniques. You live with many choices. I believe that each of you has the truth within you. I challenge you to take time on a regular basis to listen to the Spirit of Jesus. Be consistent in your choices and try not to decide upon a solution just because it is convenient. When you make a mistake, try again. Life is a process. We are always growing. I encourage you to keep growing in the direction of truth.

"Keep alive any resolutions you have made today. Try to be open to the roles of the Church, Scripture, discussion, and private prayer in developing your conscience. We will continue to pray for you. I invite you to do the same for one another. I want to close with a brief statement from Saint Paul to the people of Ephesus (Eph. 5:1–2): 'Be imitators of God as his dear children. Follow the way of love, even as Christ loved you.' "

3:30 p.m. Departure

What to Consider Before the Retreat

The introduction to this manual contains useful information about what to consider in advance of a retreat. The reader is here referred to that material, and specific additions for this retreat are also noted below.

Details in advance: See pages 11–12.

Personnel needed: See page 12.

Agenda for the staff preretreat planning meeting: See page 12. When planning the liturgy, consider using the following readings.
- First reading—1 Cor. 10:23–24,31–11:1
- Responsorial psalm—Ps. 26:4–5,6–7,8–9,11–12, with the antiphon "Your ways, O Lord, make known to me; teach me your paths."
- Gospel—Matt. 6:19–21

You may use the "Planning Sheet for Eucharistic Liturgy" on page 107 to prepare for this liturgy.

Materials needed: See page 12. In addition, bring a Bible for each retreatant. The handouts that follow should be reproduced in advance, with each handout on its own page.

Conscience Prayer

Loving God,
It is good for us to be here today.
We have taken time away from our busy schedules
    in order to reflect upon your guidance within our lives.

We face a variety of pressures.
Often, we are encouraged to take a path that does not lead to you.
We are willing to examine our lives today.
We depend upon your loving guidance.
You are the Way and the Truth and the Life.

We ask you to make your ways known to us.
Teach us your path and guide us in your truth.
We believe that with your help,
    we can learn to live our lives as loving Christians.
We pray this in the name of our Lord, Jesus.
Amen.

Looking into the Heart: A Scriptural Search

Directions: Prayerfully read and reflect upon the following scriptural passages, and write your reflections below.

• Job 27:6, "My heart does not reproach me for any of my days . . ."

• Psalm 95:8, "Harden not your hearts . . ."

• Psalm 95:10, "They are a people of erring heart . . ."

• Proverbs 2:2, "Inclining your heart to understanding . . ."

• Proverbs 4:21, "Keep them within your heart . . ."

• Proverbs 7:3, "Write them on the tablet of your heart . . ."

• Ecclesiastes 7:22, "You know in your heart . . ."

• Ezekiel 11:19–21, "I will give them a new heart . . ."

• Matthew 5:8, "Blest are the single-hearted for they shall see God . . ."

• Matthew 15:8, "This people pays me lip service but their heart is far from me . . ."

Part B
Overnight Retreats

Retreat 5 ("Values"), the first of three overnight retreats, is designed for older (eleventh- and twelfth-grade) retreatants. The program provides the opportunity for the retreatants to examine past influences and attitudes that have led them to value certain things over others. They also look at how they might integrate Christlike values into their lives. This retreat can be used as a mandatory program.

Retreat 6 ("Prayer") is designed for older (eleventh- and twelfth-grade) retreatants. During this retreat the participants examine their beliefs and attitudes toward prayer, and they experience various ways to pray. Because of the need for focused cooperation by all, it is important that the retreatants have freely chosen to attend this retreat.

Retreat 7 ("Parent-Teen Relationships [Overnight Version]") is for pairs that consist of a teenaged retreatant with a parent. The pair could be a daughter-mother, daughter-father, son-mother, or son-father couple. The teen and parent couple have the opportunity to spend time together. The program includes playful, prayerful, relaxed, and serious times. Because of the importance of this type of program, a similar parent-teen program is offered as a weekend retreat (see Retreat 9).

The retreatants themselves plan the eucharistic liturgies for the overnight and weekend liturgies. In the Appendix on pages 103–107, "Eucharistic Liturgy Preparation for Overnight and Weekend Retreats," are descriptions of the committees that work on the liturgy and instructions for presenting the session on liturgy preparation.

Retreat 5
Values

Goals

The retreat "Values" is a two-day program designed for twenty to fifty people. It has been used with eleventh- and twelfth-grade retreatants.

The goals of the retreat are the following:

1. The retreatants will examine their personal values in relation to the values lived out by Jesus.
2. The retreatants will discuss their own beliefs regarding current moral issues.
3. The retreatants will discuss the specific actions of daily life that express their personal values and beliefs.

Schedule

Day 1

10:00 a.m.	Arrival
10:30 a.m.	Introduction and prayer
11:00 a.m.	Icebreakers
11:45 a.m.	Small group 1
12:30 p.m.	Lunch
1:30 p.m.	Large group—God
1:55 p.m.	Quiet time
2:15 p.m.	Small group 2
3:15 p.m.	Break
3:30 p.m.	Organized recreation
4:00 p.m.	Break
4:15 p.m.	Large group—value awareness
4:45 p.m.	Small group 3
6:00 p.m.	Dinner
7:15 p.m.	Reconciliation
8:45 p.m.	Break
9:30 p.m.	Liturgy preparation
10:30 p.m.	Break
10:45 p.m.	Night prayer
11:15 p.m.	Closedown

Day 2

7:45 a.m.	Wake-up call
8:00 a.m.	Breakfast
8:45 a.m.	Cleanup
9:30 a.m.	Morning prayer
10:30 a.m.	Small group 4
12:15 p.m.	Lunch
1:30 p.m.	Liturgy
2:45 p.m.	Concretizing
3:00 p.m.	Departure

Retreat Activities: Day 1

10:00 a.m. Arrival

Two staff members welcome and register the retreatants, help them locate their rooms, and have them fill out name tags.

10:30 a.m. Introduction and prayer

Staff: two people (including one to assist with distribution of handouts)

Purposes: to lead the retreat community in prayer, to introduce the theme of the retreat, to introduce the retreat staff, and to explain guidelines for using the retreat facility

Materials needed: Handout 5–A, "Value Prayer"

Description of activities

Part 1: "Welcome to your retreat. My name is _____. Let's pause for a few moments and call upon God to be with us during these days together." Pause.

"Lord Jesus, we call upon you to walk with us during our retreat. Guide us as we step aside from our busy schedules to quiet ourselves. Help us to listen to your voice through nature, others, and Scripture. Teach us to value the things that really matter and to look to you as we learn to live out the values of a Christian life. Amen.

"I would like to make a few comments about the nature of this retreat. A retreat is a time to step aside from your everyday activities. It is a time to put things into perspective and to renew yourself. The focus of this retreat is on values. A value is something that I hold in esteem or cherish. It is important to me and very personal. Think a moment about your values. Who do you value? What do you value? Who or what in your experience has led you to these values? Does your behavior reflect your own values? [Pause.] During this retreat you will have an opportunity to examine these and other questions.

"You will have time to participate in large-group activities, some playful and some serious. At other times, you will meet in small groups for discussion. Some of the topics addressed will be the value of a relationship with God and the value of service. There will also be an opportunity to celebrate the Sacrament of Reconciliation and the eucharistic liturgy as a faith community.

"In order for you to get the most out of this retreat, I encourage you to leave behind any stereotypes you may have. Give others a chance to show who they truly are. Try to trust yourself, the other retreatants, the staff, and the program. Perhaps the most important encouragement I offer you is to take responsibility for fully participating in each of the activities. Your efforts will add to the quality of your experience."

Distribute Handout 5–A. "Let's join together in asking God to be with us as we say the 'Value Prayer.' " Explain which side will be the left and which the right. Read from the handout together.

Part 2: See part 2 of the "Description of activities" on page 14 of Retreat 1 for the introductions and the practical details. At the conclusion, invite the retreatants to the location for the icebreakers.

11:00 a.m. Icebreakers

Staff: one person

Purpose: to help the retreatants feel more at ease with one another

Materials needed: none

Description of activities

1. Birth dates: Tell the retreatants to stand and form one large circle, lining up in the order of the month in which their birth dates fall. Begin with January. After they have formed the circle, ask them to call out in order their birth dates. At the end, point out the importance of cooperation and listening in helping make this activity successful.

2. Music: Tell the retreatants to stand and form one large circle, lining up in alphabetical order according to the first letter of the name of their favorite musical entertainer or group. After they have formed the circle, ask them to call out in turn the name of their favorite musical entertainer or group. At the end, point out the importance of acceptance in this activity.

3. Machines: Divide the retreatants into groups of eight, with each group in a different part of the room. Ask each group to create a machine. Machines have moving parts and sounds that come from each part. Each member of the group is to actively participate. When each group presents its machine to the large group, one person at a time comes to the center of the room and joins the other group members as the machine is being created. The large group then tries to guess what machine has been created by the small group. At the end, point out the importance of participation by all in this activity.

4. Summary: After the icebreakers, tell the retreatants to be seated. Talk a little about how cooperation, listening, acceptance, and participation by all were needed for the success of the icebreakers. These same qualities are needed during the whole retreat and specifically during the small-group meetings. Explain that soon they will be going to their small groups. Encourage them to take the same cooperation and acceptance to their groups. For the first group meeting, use the groups that were already formed for creating machines. Explain the locations of the meeting rooms. Ask the retreatants to go directly to their small group's meeting room.

11:45 a.m. Small group 1

Staff: one person for each small group

Purposes: to assist the retreatants in establishing small-group discussion rules, to encourage the retreatants to set a personal goal for the retreat, and to facilitate a discussion of their own values

Materials needed for each group: an index card and a pencil for each retreatant, three large pieces of butcher paper, and a felt-tip marker

Description of activities

1. Introduction (10 min.): "I would like to begin with simple introductions. We will go around the circle. As you introduce yourself, please tell us your name and why you chose to join this retreat. After a person has been introduced, please feel free to respond or to ask questions you might have regarding the person's introductory comments." Proceed with introductions. Encourage the retreatants to talk freely about their reasons for attending the retreat.

2. Guidelines (5 min.): "During this retreat we will meet in small groups four times. These discussions are meant to give you a chance to articulate your questions and ideas, as well as to expose you to the thinking of others. Before we do begin the discussion, I would like for you to establish some guidelines. What adds to a good discussion? I will write down the guidelines you decide upon and hang them on the wall so we can refer to them if necessary." With the felt-tip marker, write the guidelines on the butcher paper. Make sure the following are included: confidentiality, respect, no put-downs, honesty, and an attempt to participate by all.

3. Personal goals (5 min.): "When you introduced yourself, you spoke briefly about your reason for coming on the retreat. Could you set a goal for yourself for the retreat? I would like you to write down a goal and then refer to it throughout the retreat. The time goes quickly, and it is easy to lose the focus." Pass out the pencils and the index cards.

4. Discussion (20 min.): Encourage the retreatants to participate in the discussion of the questions suggested below. If the group is reluctant to discuss, pair each retreatant with another person for a two-minute dyad on one question. Then return to the group discussion. Make sure the guidelines are observed. Be flexible. If the discussion seems to move in an unexpected direction, be open to the needs of the retreatants. The butcher paper can be used to record the answers to the first three questions.

• What is a definition for *value?*
• What influences a person's values?
• What do you value?
• What in your experience has led you to value this?
• Who do you value?
• What in your experience has led you to value the relationship?

5. Summary (5 min.): "Thank you for trusting each other. Before we finish the discussion, does anyone have a comment to make to the group?" Give everyone a chance to comment.

6. Closure: End with a closing prayer and explain the schedule for the afternoon.

12:30 p.m.   Lunch

One staff person is available to make announcements and to choose a retreatant to lead the group in grace before the meal.

1:30 p.m.   Large group—God

Staff: two people (including one to assist with distributing the handouts, operating the tape recorder, and supervising the quiet time)

Purposes: to invite the retreatants to reflect upon their relationships with God and to introduce the value of quiet time

Materials needed: Handout 5–B, "Quiet-Time Questions About God"; a pencil for each retreatant; a tape recorder; and a tape of instrumental music

Description of activities

1. Introduction: "In your small group before lunch, you talked about some of your values. At this time, I invite you to reflect upon your relationship with God. Is this relationship of value to you? Who are some of the people and what are some of the experiences that have influenced you in this area?

"To assist you in thinking about your experience, I want to briefly share my own story. My story is simple. There is nothing spectacular about it. However, it is mine, and it has taught me certain things. As I tell of my personal experience, be thinking of your own. Afterward, you will have some quiet time alone to reflect."

2. Presentation: Tell your own story to the retreatants, using the following outline as a guide.
a. Name some of the people who have influenced you in your relationship with God (e.g., mom, dad, teacher, friend), and explain how they influenced you.
b. Tell of some positive and negative experiences that have influenced you in your relationship with God (e.g., praying together as a family, a death, religious education classes).
c. Name some of the images of God you have had over the years (e.g., Friend, Loving Parent, Judge, Police Officer, Pain Reliever).
d. Explain what your relationship with God means to you now.

Your honesty will be an invitation to the retreatants to examine their own stories. Keep your statements simple and clear. This may be an emotional presentation because of the personal witnessing it entails. Keep in mind that you are trying to help the retreatants become more aware of their own stories.

3. Conclusion: "This is a very personal topic. I hope by telling my story, you have thought about your own experiences. For some of you, the relationship you have with God is important. For others of you it is not. Claim your own story. Examine where you are and where you want to be in this area."

4. Introduction to quiet time: "During the next twenty minutes, I invite you to reflect on your story. Please take the 'Quiet-Time Questions About God' and a pencil. Find a quiet place to be alone. Write any reflections you have. There will be quiet music playing in this room. After twenty minutes, please return to this room. You will divide into small groups to talk about your reflections."

Pass out the pencils and Handout 5–B, and turn on the music. Then invite all to find a quiet place to be alone. Both the leader and the assistant should supervise the retreatants during the quiet time. After twenty minutes, call the retreatants back into the room. Divide them into small groups and direct them to their small group's meeting room.

1:55 p.m. Quiet time

2:15 p.m. Small group 2

Staff: one person for each small group

Purpose: to facilitate a discussion on valuing a relationship with God

Materials needed: none

Description of activities

1. Introduction (10 min.): Ask the retreatants to introduce themselves to the group. Remind them of the guidelines established during the first small group. Ask each person to explain his or her feelings about discussing the topic of valuing a relationship with God.

2. Discussion (40 min.): Invite the retreatants to talk about their experiences of God, using the handout "Quiet-Time Questions About God." Encourage them to be honest. There might be some initial resistance to discussing this topic. Respect each person's feelings.

3. Summary (10 min.): "Thank you for your honesty and for trusting one another. You are the first generation of the 'new' Church. You were born after the Vatican II renewal began. Trust that the Holy Spirit speaks to you. Take time to examine the truth as you know it. Believe in yourself. Your perspective will be different from that of others who are older than you because each of you has had different experiences. Respect one another. Try to find the best in the past and in the present. Before we close this session, does anyone have anything you would like to say to the group?" Allow each person to make a closing statement.

4. Closure: Invite a retreatant to lead the group in a closing prayer.

3:15 p.m. Break

3:30 p.m. Organized recreation

Staff: two people

Purpose: to have the retreatants exercise and have fun as a group (e.g., by playing volleyball)

Materials needed: recreational equipment (volleyballs, footballs, Frisbees, etc.)

4:00 p.m. Break

4:15 p.m. Large group—value awareness

Staff: one person

Purpose: to challenge the retreatants to take a stand on current moral issues

Materials needed: value-awareness signs "Strongly Agree" and "Strongly Disagree," and four carpet squares

Description of activities

Before beginning this activity, hang the signs "Strongly Agree" and "Strongly Disagree" at opposite ends of the room. Space the four carpet squares on the floor, from the "Strongly Agree" position to the "Strongly Disagree" position.

1. Background on values: "So far, during this retreat you have had the opportunity to see yourself in relationship to other people. This happened in a very simple way during the icebreakers when you lined up by date of birth. Then in the first small group, you defined 'values.' During the talk about valuing God, you had the opportunity to listen to the presenter speak of his [her] experience. In listening, we hope that you started to think about your own experience of God. And you had a chance to speak about your own experience of God in a small group.

"Throughout this retreat, I hope that you get closer to discovering a set of values—that you identify the values you already have. This next activity and the discussion following is meant to help you learn more about yourself; become more aware of your beliefs, attitudes, and feelings; and look more clearly at what it is that you value.

"My values are continually changing; they are never static. As I reevaluate myself in relation to the world, I rechoose my values. As I grow, I rechoose my values. As a child, I first saw myself in relation to my mother, my father, my brothers and sisters, and later in relation to the school and society. As I reevaluated myself in relation to each of these, I made fresh choices: I developed a value system. When I say that I truly value something, I mean that this valuing is a total stance as expressed through my behavior, ideas, feelings, and imagination.

"Then there is the ranking of values. When there is a conflict between two people, I usually find that one person is trying to force the other to accept his or her ranking of values. For instance, a teenager and a parent may both value schoolwork, sports, friends, and the parent-child relationship. However the teenager may rank them in this way: no. 1—friends, no. 2—sports, no. 3—schoolwork, and no. 4—parent-child relationship. The parent may rank them in this way: no. 1 – parent-child relationship, no. 2 – schoolwork, no. 3 – sports, and no. 4 – friends. You will probably find that you have different values from some other persons in your small group. On the other hand, you may find that you agree with these same people on other values.

"Try to clarify your values. Where are your values in relation to those for which Jesus stood: peace, patience, forgiveness, tolerance, generosity, service, and unconditional love? Are there any of Jesus' values that you would like to integrate into your own life? Please be thinking about this as we proceed through this activity.

"For some of you, this might be the first time that you have been asked to think about or take a stand on some of the issues we'll be bringing up. For others, because of some previous experience, you have already had the opportunity to clarify your beliefs. Wherever you are in this regard, recall what I said earlier. Values are never static. They are continually changing. As I grow, I rechoose my values."

2. Directions: "Here are the directions for this activity. I will read a series of statements. Some are about controversial moral issues. Others are about everyday experiences. The first time I read the statement, please remain still and think about your feelings, beliefs, and values on that issue.

"The second time I read the statement, please take a stand by walking *in silence* to the appropriate place in the room. Note that the carpet at one end of the room represents 'strongly agree,' and at the other end of the room the carpet represents 'strongly disagree.' The two carpets in the middle represent 'mildly agree' and 'mildly disagree.' There is no 'undecided' stance allowed. Everyone must take a stand by agreeing or disagreeing with the statement. Please remember, it is very important that this whole activity takes place in silence. Before we begin, do you have any questions?" Pause.

3. Value-awareness statements: Read each value-awareness statement twice, allowing time after the first reading for the retreatants to consider their reactions to the statement and time after the second reading for them to take their stands.
- Making fun of people is an acceptable form of humor.
- It is okay to use alcohol and other drugs as an escape.
- Nuclear weapons should be used if needed to protect our country.
- I can forgive anything.
- Religious teachings make little difference in the way I think and act in everyday life.
- Cheating is all right as long as you don't get caught.
- Christ would support the rights of a gay person.
- Abortion is murder.
- Premarital sex is all right as long as the people are in love.
- I will raise my children differently than my parents raised me.

After the exercise is completed, ask the retreatants to sit down. "It is likely that you felt some peer pressure while you were taking your stands. How did you respond to that pressure? Did you go along with the crowd if you could not make up your mind or if you were embarrassed about your opinion? How did you feel if at any point you were alone in your stand?"

Divide the retreatants into small groups and ask them to go directly to their group's meeting room.

4:45 p.m. Small group 3

Staff: one person for each small group

Purpose: to facilitate a discussion on current moral issues

Materials needed: none

Description of activities
1. Introduction (5 min.): Ask the retreatants to introduce themselves to the group. Remind the retreatants of the guidelines established during the first small group.

2. Discussion (60 min.): Invite the retreatants to talk about their stances taken on the various value-awareness statements. There will probably not be enough time to discuss all the issues. Begin with the issues most important to the retreatants. With each value statement discussed, encourage the retreatants to explain the following:
- What values do you uphold when you take that stance?
- What in your experience has led you to value this?

3. Summary (10 min.): Encourage the retreatants to continue to examine their values in the light of those lived out by Jesus. Invite each group member to make a closing comment to the group.

4. Closure: Invite a retreatant to lead the group in a closing prayer.

6:00 p.m. Dinner

One staff person is available to make announcements and to choose a retreatant to lead the group in grace before the meal.

7:15 p.m. Reconciliation

Staff: one leader and several priests, depending on the number of retreatants

Purpose: to invite the retreatants to receive the Sacrament of Reconciliation

Materials needed: an aluminum roasting pan, a candle, a 3-by-3-inch paper and a pencil for each retreatant, a tape recorder, and a tape of instrumental music

Description of activities

Upon entering the chapel, give each participant a pencil and a 3-by-3-inch paper. Have a candle lit near the aluminum pan.

1. Opening prayer: "We have gathered this evening for a reconciliation service. This is a time for you to take a look at your values and actions in light of the values and actions of Jesus. Please join me in an opening prayer.

"Lord, our God, you are patient with sinners and accept our desires to make amends. We acknowledge our sins and are resolved to change our lives. Help us to celebrate this sacrament of your love. We ask this through Jesus Christ, our Lord."

2. On reconciliation: "Coming from the Catholic tradition, I believe that the most important, basic value for a happy and healthy life is the value of forgiveness. Each time we profess our creed, we say that we believe in four basic areas: first, God and the many ways we experience God; second, the people of God, whether they be living or dead; third, life, now and everlasting; and fourth, the forgiveness of sins. As I look at the creed, I see that forgiveness is the only *act* in which we profess to believe.

"The sad thing for me is that so few Christians that I know are truly able to forgive others or themselves. If they could, I do believe our lives would be much happier and much more peaceful."

3. The penitent woman: "I have chosen a reading about forgiveness. Please listen to a reading from Luke's Gospel about the penitent woman." Read Luke 7:36–50.

"Because her love was so great, Jesus offered her forgiveness. This woman is one of my favorite characters in Scripture. I like to imagine being in her place. How would you feel if you were in her place? Imagine if you expressed to Jesus how much his friendship meant to you. Imagine how you would feel if someone criticized you for your expressions of love. And then how would you feel when Jesus stood up for you? For me, this is such a wonderful story of reconciliation."

4. Examination of conscience: "I invite you to spend some time now thinking about your own actions and values. I will read a list of values and questions about them. Perhaps something will remind you of areas on which you would like to work." Read the following examination of conscience.

I say I value my family . . .
- Do I show those at home that I appreciate them?
- Do I do my part to support those at home?
- Do I try to spend some quality time with my family each week?

I say I value God and my faith . . .
- Does my behavior reflect Christlike values?
- Do I take time to strengthen my relationship with God?

I say I value my friends . . .
- Do I give them freedom, or do I demand that they live up to my expectations?

- Am I there for them in bad times as well as good?

I say I value my health . . .
- Does my attitude toward my health and the choices I make reflect the care I should be giving my body?
- Do I abuse my health with alcohol or drugs or abuse the sanctity of my sexuality?

I say I value communication . . .
- Am I really open with others, or do I lie and act phony?
- Do I tell others what I really feel, or do I remain quiet because it is easier and safer?
- Am I honest with myself?

Are there other areas where my thoughts, words, and actions have not reflected my values?

"Each of you has a paper and a pencil. As you reflect, write on the paper one area in which you need forgiveness. Later you will have a chance to burn this paper. Let the burning be a reminder of how our sins are forgotten when they are consumed by God's love." Pause for three minutes. Soft instrumental music may be played in the background.

5. Confessions: "At this time we would like to offer you the chance to be reconciled with God and with each other through the Sacrament of Reconciliation. Try to look at this sacrament today as a sign of God's love. Instead of focusing on what you tell the priest, focus on the reminder of God's loving forgiveness spoken through the words of the priest."

Indicate to the retreatants the priest(s) who will be hearing confessions. If there is more than one priest available for the sacrament, tell the retreatants the location of each. Let them know that if they wish to discuss something in greater depth than time allows, the priest will be available later as well. Explain that they have the option of going to confession for the sacrament, simply asking the priest for a blessing, or asking him to pray with them for a particular concern.

"After meeting with Father, light your paper from the candle and place your paper in the pan."

6. Reconciling with one another: "While people are seeing Father, I encourage you to go around the room and speak to others one-on-one. Try to talk with as many people as possible. When you meet each other, either offer some words of support or thanks, or ask for forgiveness if you need to. Music will be on in the background and the lights will be dimmed to give you a sense of privacy." Turn on the instrumental music.

7. Closing: For a closing prayer, invite the retreatants to form a circle and join in praying the Lord's Prayer.

8:45 p.m. Break

9:30 p.m. Liturgy preparation

See the Appendix, pages 103–107, for a full explanation of the work of the committees and instructions for presenting the session on liturgy preparation to the retreatants.

10:30 p.m. Break

10:45 p.m. Night prayer

Staff: two people (including one to assist with the tape recorder)

Purpose: to invite the retreatants to offer a prayer of thanks

Materials needed: a candle, a tape recorder, and a tape with an appropriate song (e.g., "Sometimes" by the Carpenters)

Description of activities

"Welcome to our night prayer. It has been a long day for you. You have met many new people. You have examined some of your values. You have reconciled yourself with God and others. As a way of closing our day, I offer you the opportunity to express a prayer of thanks. For whom are you thankful? For what are you thankful? Reflect on this as I play a song entitled 'Sometimes' that the Carpenters sang a number of years ago." Turn on the music.

"I will pass this candle around the circle. When it comes to you, offer your prayer of thanks. If you do not wish to pray out loud, then simply hold the candle and offer your prayer quietly. After offering your prayer, pass the candle on to the next person. As others are offering their prayers, try to join them in prayer by listening attentively."

Begin by offering a prayer: "Lord, thank you for . . ." Pass the candle to the first retreatant. If the group seems timid, before you begin the prayer, tell the retreatant sitting next to you to be prepared to offer a prayer of thanks. It is easier when the first person is prepared. This will serve as a model for the others. After the candle has been passed around the circle, close by inviting all to pray the Glory Be as a prayer of praise.

11:15 p.m. Closedown

One person announces the time for lights out, the second day's schedule, and any other information.

Retreat Activities: Day 2

7:45 a.m. Wake-up call

8:00 a.m. Breakfast

8:45 a.m. Cleanup

Staff: one person

Purposes: to instruct the retreatants on the expectations for preparing for departure and to provide the time for the retreatants to change sheets, clean rooms, pack, and load the cars or the bus

Materials needed: none

9:30 a.m. Morning prayer

Staff: two people (including one to assist with distributing the Bibles)

Purpose: to invite the retreatants to prayerfully reflect on Jesus' words and actions as found in Scripture

Materials needed: a Bible for each retreatant

Description of activities

"Good morning! As we begin our day, let us prayerfully place ourselves in the presence of God." Pause.

"As Christians we profess to be followers of Jesus. Jesus' actions and words indicate his values just as ours do. Jesus spoke of forgiveness; Jesus acted generously; Jesus offered unconditional love. In clarifying our own values, I believe it is important to examine ours in light of those lived out by Jesus. Only then are we able to truly follow Jesus.

"I encourage you to examine your words and actions. Look at those of Jesus. What do you need to do in order to follow Jesus' example more closely? For the next twenty minutes, you may go outside and find a quiet place to reflect on this. Take a Bible with you. Note especially chapters 5, 6, 7, and 8 of Matthew's Gospel. What is Jesus saying? What is Jesus doing? After twenty minutes, please return to the chapel, and we will share some of our insights."

Pass out the Bibles. Invite the retreatants to find a quiet place to be alone. The leader and the assistant should be available to supervise the retreatants. After twenty minutes, call them back to the chapel. Ask the retreatants to turn to another person and share their insights. Close the morning prayer by reading Phil. 1:9–11. Divide the retreatants into small groups and explain the location of the small-group meeting rooms.

10:30 a.m. Small group 4

Staff: one person for each small group

Purposes: to facilitate a discussion on resolutions the retreatants may be making and to invite them to affirm one another

Materials needed: none

Description of activities

1. Introduction (10 min.): Ask the retreatants to introduce themselves to the group. Remind the retreatants of the guidelines established during the first small group. Invite each person to share any reflections from the morning prayer.

2. Resolutions (25 min.): Divide the retreatants into pairs. Ask them to discuss the questions suggested below with their partners. After five to ten minutes, have them change partners. Do this two more times. Then invite them to talk to the group about any resolutions they wish to make.

- What are your talents?
- How do you use your time?
- What are some of your material possessions?
- What do you value?
- In order to live out your values, what do you wish to change regarding
  a. how you use your talents?
  b. how you use your time?
  c. how you share your material possessions?

3. Goals (10 min.): Invite each retreatant to state the goal he or she had for the retreat and to explain whether or not the goal was accomplished.

4. Affirmation (45 min.): Invite the retreatants to speak to one another about the values they appreciate in one another. Choose a person with whom to start and ask each group member to speak directly to that person, stating specific values he or she sees lived out in the person. After the person has been affirmed, allow him or her the opportunity to make a statement to the group.

5. Summary (10 min.): Thank the retreatants for their honesty and for trusting one another. Ask if anyone has any statement that he or she would like to say to the group. Go around the circle, allowing each person the opportunity to make a closing statement.

6. Closure: Invite a retreatant to lead the group in a closing prayer.

12:15 p.m. Lunch

One staff person is available to make announcements and to choose a retreatant to lead the group in grace before the meal.

1:30 p.m. Liturgy

The committees carry out those parts of the liturgy for which they are responsible.

2:45 p.m. Concretizing

Staff: one person

Purposes: to remind the retreatants of the retreat theme and to challenge them to keep alive any commitments or resolutions made during the retreat

Materials needed: none

Description of activities

"Take a moment now to reflect on your current feelings. You are the person responsible for these feelings. If you feel good about the retreat experience, you are the person to thank, since you did the work. We simply provided an atmosphere.

"I encourage you to take home and put into action any resolutions you have made for yourself. Try to integrate into your life the values you lived while on retreat. Some of the things you lived were quiet reflection, reconciliation, praying with Scripture, playfulness, taking a stand on moral issues, and respect for others. Try to model your behavior after the example of Jesus.

"We will continue to pray for you. Please do the same for one another. We sincerely thank you for your cooperation. I invite you to go now to one another and offer some sign of thanks."

3:00 p.m. Departure

What to Consider Before the Retreat

The introduction to this manual contains useful information about what to consider in advance of a retreat. The reader is here referred to that material, and specific additions for this retreat are also noted below.

Details in advance: See pages 11–12.

Personnel needed: See page 12.

Agenda for the staff preretreat planning meeting: See page 12. On dividing the retreatants into small groups, note that during this retreat, the retreatants could meet with four different small groups. This would entail dividing the large group up four times, once for each small-group meeting. The advantage of meeting with different groups rather than one small group throughout is that it gives the retreatants an opportunity to get to know most of the other retreatants.

Materials needed: See page 12.

In addition, for *liturgy preparation,* bring decoration supplies (crayons, scissors, glue, tape, construction paper, pencils, a ruler, and a large piece of butcher paper).

Miscellaneous materials needed are an aluminum roasting pan (for the reconciliation service), two value-awareness signs ("Strongly Agree" and "Strongly Disagree"), four carpet squares, and a 3-by-3-inch paper for each retreatant.

The handouts that follow should be reproduced in advance, with each handout on its own page.

All: Lord, it is good for us to be here together. It is together that we live out the values in our lives.

Right: We value time. Make us aware of the importance of taking time with you and with one another. We seem to be so busy doing that often we forget simply to "be."

Left: We value our sight. Clear our eyes so that we might break the stereotypes we have of people, which keep them in chains instead of leading them to freedom.

Right: We value listening. Help us to listen not only with our ears but also with our hearts so that we might heal the wounds that have separated us.

Left: We value ourselves. Let us discover once again the unique qualities that have been given to us through our creation. Let us live out these qualities so that we can help create a new world: a world of peace, a world of truth, and a world of justice.

All: We are your instruments, Lord. We are the hope of a better world if we live out the values of a Christian life. We ask your blessing and your abiding presence during this retreat as we rethink and re-create values that will help us to love one another as we love you.

Quiet-Time Questions About God

Directions: Read and reflect on the following questions about God. Then write your reflections below (and on the reverse side of this handout, if necessary).

• Who are some of the people who have influenced you about God? How have they influenced you?

• What are some of the images that you have had of God over the years? That is, how have you pictured God at different times in your life?

• What experiences have you had that have changed these images? What experiences (positive or negative) have affected your relationship with God?

• Who is God for you now? Is your relationship with God a value in your life?

Permission to reproduce this handout is granted.

Retreat 6
Prayer

Goals

The retreat "Prayer" has been designed for older (eleventh- and twelfth-grade) retreatants. It is a two-day program for twenty-five to forty-five participants.

The goals of the retreat are the following:
1. The retreatants will examine their beliefs, feelings, and attitudes toward prayer.
2. The retreatants will experience various ways to pray.
3. The retreatants will examine ways to include prayer in their daily schedules.

Schedule

Day 1

10:00 a.m.	Arrival
10:15 a.m.	Introduction and prayer
10:45 a.m.	Small group 1
11:30 a.m.	Letter writing
12:15 p.m.	Lunch
1:00 p.m.	Organized recreation
2:00 p.m.	Quiet time
2:45 p.m.	Small group 2
4:00 p.m.	Break
4:30 p.m.	Liturgy preparation
5:45 p.m.	Dinner
7:00 p.m.	Reconciliation
8:30 p.m.	Break
9:15 p.m.	Songfest
10:15 p.m.	Break
10:30 p.m.	Night prayer
11:00 p.m.	Closedown

Day 2

8:00 a.m.	Wake-up call
8:30 a.m.	Breakfast
9:15 a.m.	Cleanup
10:00 a.m.	Morning prayer
11:15 a.m.	Break
11:30 a.m.	Small group 3
12:15 p.m.	Lunch
1:30 p.m.	Liturgy
2:45 p.m.	Concretizing
3:00 p.m.	Departure

Retreat Activities: Day 1

10:00 a.m. Arrival

Two staff members welcome and register the retreatants, help them locate their rooms, and have them fill out name tags.

10:15 a.m. Introduction and prayer

Staff: two people (including one to assist with the distribution of handouts)

Purposes: to lead the retreat community in prayer, to introduce the theme of the retreat, to introduce the retreat staff, and to explain guidelines for using the retreat facility

Materials needed: a Bible and Handout 6–A, "A Prayer of Trust and Thanks"

Description of activities

Part 1: "Welcome to your retreat. My name is _____. Before we begin, let's pause for a few minutes and call upon God to be with us during these days together." Pause.

"Lord Jesus, we call upon you to guide us throughout these days of prayer. So often you took time away from the crowd in order to pray. Be our teacher so that we can grow in our relationship with our loving God. We offer our prayer in your name, Lord Jesus. Amen.

"I would like to make a few comments about the nature of this retreat. A retreat is a time to step aside from your busy schedule in order to grow in your relationship with God. The theme for this retreat is 'prayer.' Prayer is communication with God. This includes speaking as well as listening. There are numerous ways to pray and a variety of types of prayer. Some examples are the prayer of silence, vocal prayer, the Jesus prayer, the rosary, and communal prayer. And a prayer can be one of praise, thanks, petition, or contrition. During these days of retreat, you will have the opportunity to experience various ways to pray.

"The success of this retreat greatly depends on your willingness to try each activity. Give an extra effort if you find an activity to be difficult. We are not able to teach you how to pray. We can only provide you the opportunity to experience it. I encourage you to be supportive of one another by praying for others throughout the retreat. Use your break time for reading, reflection, or recreation. Try to respond to what you need at this time."

Distribute Handout 6–A. "Before I introduce our staff to you, please join in praying 'A Prayer of Trust and Thanks,' which is Ps. 16." Explain which sides are right and left. Read from the handout together.

Part 2: See part 2 of the "Description of activities" on page 14 of Retreat 1 for the introductions and the practical details. At the conclusion, invite the retreatants to the location for the next activity.

10:45 a.m. Small group 1

Staff: one person for each small group

Purposes: to create an environment where the retreatants feel comfortable to share their thoughts and feelings, to have the retreatants set a goal to be worked toward during the reteat, to have them discuss their own prayer life, and to introduce the activity of letter writing

Materials needed for each group: three large pieces of butcher paper, a felt-tip marker, masking tape, a pencil and two pieces of 8½-by-11-inch paper for each retreatant

Description of activities

1. Introduction (10 min.): "Let's begin with some simple introductions. As we go around the circle, please tell us your name and the reason why you decided to attend this retreat." As the retreatants introduce themselves, encourage them to respond to one another in some way.

2. Guidelines (5 min.): "During this retreat we will meet as a small group three times. These discussions are meant to give you a chance to articulate your questions and ideas as well as to expose you to the thinking of others. Before we do begin the discussion, I would like you to establish some guidelines for discussion. What adds to a good discussion? I will write down the guidelines as you name them. I will hang them on the wall so we can refer to them when necessary." With the felt-tip marker, write the guidelines on the butcher paper. Make sure the following are included: confidentiality, respect, no put-downs, honesty, trust, and an attempt to participate by all.

3. Personal goals (5 min.): "When you introduced yourself, you spoke briefly about your reason for joining the retreat. Could you set a goal for yourself for the retreat? The time goes quickly, and it is easy to lose the focus. After you decide upon a goal, please tell the group. I will list it on the butcher paper. During our final small group, we will refer to the list." Write the goals on the butcher paper. Post these on the wall.

4. Discussion (20 min.): Encourage the retreatants to participate in the discussion of the questions suggested below. Remind the retreatants of the guidelines, if necessary.
- What is your attitude toward prayer?
- When do you pray?
- How do you pray?
- What prevents you from praying more often?
- What are obstacles to prayer for you?
- What about prayer is easy for you?
- What about prayer is difficult for you?
- What hope do you have for your prayer life in the future?

5. Explanation of letter writing (5 min.): "Thank you for trusting each other. I encourage you to take some time alone now to reflect upon what has been said. As an experience of one type of prayer or communication with God, I invite you to write a letter to Jesus. In Mark's Gospel (Mark 10:46–52), Jesus speaks to a blind man and asks, 'What do you want me to do for you?' Imagine that Jesus is asking you this same question: 'What do you want me to do for you?' In your letter, respond to Jesus asking this question of you. Take your time and reflect on what you would say. Find a place by yourself. Then write your letter. You have plenty of time, since lunch is not until 12:15 p.m. Please return your pencil to the box located in the dining room. Put your letter in a safe place so that you can refer to it later. Do you have any questions?" Pass out the pencils and the paper.

11:30 a.m. Letter writing

12:15 p.m. Lunch

One staff person is available to make announcements and to choose a retreatant to lead the group in grace before the meal.

1:00 p.m. Organized recreation

Staff: two people

Purpose: to encourage the retreatants to find prayer in the playfulness of a volleyball game

Materials needed: two volleyballs

2:00 p.m. Quiet time

Staff: two people, including one to assist with the tape recorder and the slide projector

Purpose: to introduce the retreatants to the value of taking time for quiet prayer

Materials needed: a Bible, a tape of a quiet song, a tape recorder, a slide projector, a screen, and slides of nature

Description of activities

Have the slide projector and screen set up in the chapel, with the slides of nature ready to present.

"Already you have experienced two ways to pray. We prayed Ps. 16 together as a faith community during our introductory gathering, and before lunch you wrote a letter to Jesus responding to a question posed by him in Scripture.

"This afternoon I invite you to participate in a prayer of quiet. I will show you some slides of nature to help you relax and quiet yourselves. After the slides are presented, try to quiet your body and your mind. Breathe slowly and deeply. Empty yourself and quietly sit in the presence of God. Know that Jesus is present to you in a very special way in the Holy Eucharist reserved in the tabernacle. Rest in the quiet presence of the Lord. If you have a difficult time quieting yourself, please respect the efforts of others. We'll be quiet for about a half hour."

Show the slides of nature. Play a quiet song during the slides. Remain still after the slides are presented. At 2:40 p.m., gently invite the retreatants to bring their thoughts back to the chapel.

2:45 p.m. Small group 2

Staff: one person for each small group

Purposes: to encourage the retreatants to talk about their responses to the retreat so far and to invite them to enjoy the beauty of nature with a partner and then discuss the experience of this "nature walk"

Materials needed: none

Description of activities

1. Introduction (15 min.): Ask the retreatants to quietly review the personal goals that they set at the beginning of the retreat. Encourage them to talk with one another about their responses toward the three types of prayer already experienced. These include the communal reading of Psalm 16, the letter to Jesus, and the prayer of quiet.

2. "Nature walk" (30 min.): Invite the group members to participate in a prayer of praise—a "nature walk." Divide the group members into pairs. Invite the retreatants as pairs to explore the beauty of nature using all their senses (sight, hearing, smell, touch, and taste). Ask them to help each other explore the beauty, while being careful not to distract other pairs. Have them return to the group after twenty-five minutes.

3. Discussion (20 min.): Encourage the retreatants to participate in the discussion of the questions suggested below. Remind them of the guidelines, if necessary.

- What was difficult for you during this activity?
- What was easy for you during this activity?
- What did you see? smell? taste? touch? hear?
- How did you feel during this activity?
- How has this affected your attitude toward prayer?
- How has this affected your attitude toward the Creator?

4. Summary (10 min.): Thank the retreatants for their honesty and for trusting each other. Encourage them to continue to keep their senses open to the magnificent beauty that surrounds them in nature. Explain that this openness to nature is one of the universal ways to pray, and that being close to nature brings us back to the essential things about life and the beauty of creation. Also express your appreciation for their willingness to help each other explore nature and for their beauty as individuals. Before ending the group, go around the circle, allowing each person to make a closing statement.

5. Closure: Invite a retreatant to lead the group in a closing prayer.

4:00 p.m. Break

4:30 p.m. Liturgy preparation

See the Appendix, pages 103–107, for a full explanation of the work of the committees and instructions for presenting the session on liturgy preparation to the retreatants.

5:45 p.m. Dinner

One staff person is available to make announcements and to ask a retreatant to lead the group in grace before the meal.

7:00 p.m. Reconciliation

Staff: a leader and several priests, depending upon the number of retreatants

Purpose: to invite the retreatants to receive the Sacrament of Reconciliation

Materials needed: a Bible, a small candle for each retreatant, an Easter candle, a sandbox, a tape recorder, and a tape with appropriate songs

Description of activities

As the retreatants enter the chapel, give each of them a small candle. Have the sandbox placed near the Easter candle.

1. The Good Shepherd: "We have gathered this evening for a reconciliation service. The Sacrament of Reconciliation offers us a time to strengthen and to renew our relationship with God and others. Often in Scripture we are called to return to the Lord. God is patient and loving and waits for our return." Read Luke 15:1–7.

"Let the Good Shepherd carry you home. Feel his strong and gentle hands holding you close to himself. Know the desire of the Lord to be in a loving relationship with you."

2. Examination of conscience: "Take some time now to reflect upon areas in your life where the Lord is absent. I will read a list of questions. Perhaps something will touch your experience." Read the following examination of conscience.

- Is my life directed toward loving God, or is personal greed the object of my devotion?
- Do I take sufficient time to pray each day?
- Do I take steps to deepen my understanding of my faith?
- Do I show reverence to God in my speech?
- Do I use others to gain my own interests?
- Do I show affection to my family?
- Am I patient with my family and friends?
- Do I deal honestly with others?
- Do I promote Christian values?

Pause. Play soft music for a few minutes.

3. Confessions: "At this time we would like to offer you the chance to be reconciled with God and with each other through the Sacrament of Reconciliation."

Indicate to the retreatants the priest[s] who will be hearing confessions. If there is more than one priest available for the sacrament, tell the retreatants where each will be located. Explain that they have the option of going to confession for the sacrament, of simply asking the priest for a blessing, or of asking him to pray with them for a particular concern.

"After speaking with the priest, bring your small candle to the Easter candle. Light your candle and place it in the sandbox as a sign of your renewed relationship with the Lord and your desire to walk in the light of the Lord."

4. Reconciling with one another: "While others are seeing the priest, I encourage you to go around the room and speak to others to offer support, thanks, or reconciliation. Music will be played in the background and the lights will be dimmed in order to give you a sense of privacy. Before we begin, does anyone have any questions?"

Dim the lights and play soft music.

5. Closing: For a closing prayer, invite the retreatants to form a circle and join in praying the Lord's Prayer.

8:30 p.m. Break

9:15 p.m. Songfest

Staff: one person (a musician, especially a musically talented retreatant)

Purpose: to encourage the retreatants to participate in a songfest as another way to pray

Materials needed: songbooks (For religious music, the parish or school's liturgical songbooks could be used; for contemporary popular songs, students could be asked to bring their tapes or records. Suggested popular "classics" are listed in the "Resources" on pages 108–109.)

Description of activities
Gather the retreatants in a comfortable room. Pass out the songbooks. Allow them to choose the songs to be sung.

10:15 p.m. Break

10:30 p.m. Night prayer

Staff: two people

Purposes: to create an atmosphere in which the retreatants can reflect on how others have been supportive of them and to provide the retreatants with the opportunity to voice a prayer of thanks

Materials needed: a Bible, a candle, a tape recorder, and an appropriate tape (e.g., "Without Your Love" by Roger Daltry)

Description of activities
Have a candle placed in front of the leader.

"Welcome to our night prayer. It has been a long day for you. You have met many new people. You have experienced various ways to pray, including quiet time, praise, and reconciliation. As a way of closing our day I offer you the opportunity to express a prayer of thanks. For whom are you thankful? For what are you thankful? Reflect on this as I play the song 'Without Your Love' by Roger Daltry." Play the song.

"Notice that I have a candle burning in front of me. For ages, fire has been a sign of the presence of God. The sanctuary lamp burns to remind us of Jesus' presence in the Eucharist. Let this candle be that same reminder to you of the nearness of God.

"I will pass the candle around the circle. When it comes to you, offer your prayer of thanks. If you do not wish to pray out loud, then simply hold the candle and offer your prayer quietly. After offering your prayer, pass the candle on to the next person. As others are offering their prayers, try to join with them in prayer by listening attentively."

Begin by offering a prayer: "Lord, thank you for . . ." Pass the candle to the first retreatant. If the group seems timid, before you begin the prayer tell the retreatant sitting next to you to be prepared to offer a prayer of thanks. It is easier when the first person is prepared.

This will serve as a model for the others. After the candle has been passed around the circle, close by inviting all to pray the Glory Be as a prayer of praise.

11:00 p.m. Closedown

One person explains the schedule for the next day and makes other announcements.

Retreat Activities: Day 2

8:00 a.m. Wake-up call

8:30 a.m. Breakfast

9:15 a.m. Cleanup

Staff: one person

Purposes: to instruct the retreatants on the expectations for preparing for departure and to provide the time for the retreatants to change sheets, clean rooms, pack, and load the cars or the bus

Materials needed: none

10:00 a.m. Morning prayer

Staff: two people (including one to assist with distributing the paper, the pencils, and the envelopes)

Purposes: to create an atmosphere for the retreatants to reflect on the experience of the retreat and to provide the time for them to write a letter to themselves

Materials needed: an 8½-by-11-inch piece of paper, an envelope, and a pencil for each retreatant; a Bible; a tape recorder; and a tape with appropriate music

Description of activities

Upon entering the chapel, each retreatant receives a Bible, a pencil, a piece of paper, and an envelope.

"Good morning! We begin our day with a prayer that has two parts. You will be reflecting on a reading from Scripture and also writing a letter to yourself as a reminder of what has taken place during the retreat. Listen as I read from Matthew's Gospel." Read Matt. 6:26–34.

"Jesus reminds us to trust in God and to set our sights on the Way of the Lord. If we have our hearts and minds set on his Way, all things will fall into place. In a few minutes I will give you time to reread and reflect on that passage. What does it mean to you? What is God saying to you?

"After taking an adequate amount of time to reflect on the passage, write a letter to yourself, trying to capture your insights. You began the retreat by writing a letter to Jesus. Has the letter been answered in any way? Along with recording your insights from Scripture in this letter to yourself, write about your experience of the retreat. What types of prayer do you prefer? How could you integrate prayer into your daily schedule? Be sure to take all the time you need, as the next activity does not begin until 11:30 a.m.

"Save the letter to yourself and refer to it regularly. Let it be a reminder of any resolutions you feel you need to make. Does anyone have any questions? I invite you to go now to find a quiet place. There will be quiet music playing in this room. Read and prayerfully reflect on Matt. 6:26–34. Write yourself a letter that captures your experience of the retreat." Turn on the music.

11:15 a.m. Break

11:30 a.m. Small group 3

Staff: one person for each small group

Purposes: to invite the retreatants to examine ways to integrate prayer into their daily schedules

Materials needed for each group: an 8½-by-11-inch paper and a pencil for each retreatant

Description of activities

1. Introduction (5 min.): Encourage each person to participate in the discussion. Ask the retreatants to review the guidelines and the posted goals they set at the beginning of the retreat.

2. Discussion (30 min.): Invite the retreatants to consider their experience of prayer during the retreat by discussing the questions suggested below.

- How was the retreat experience for you?
- What types of prayer do you prefer?
- What types of prayer would you like to experience yet?
- What activity was difficult for you?
- What activity was helpful to you?
- Were you able to accomplish your goal?
- How could you integrate prayer into your schedule every day?

3. Summary (10 min.): Encourage the retreatants to continue to be open to various types of prayer. Emphasize that God communicates with us in so many ways and that they should be creative in how they speak to God, as well as in how they listen. Go around the circle, allowing each person to make a statement, if he or she wishes.

4. Closure: Ask a retreatant to lead the group in a closing prayer.

12:15 p.m. Lunch

One staff person is available to make announcements and to choose a retreatant to lead the group in grace before the meal.

1:30 p.m. Liturgy

The committees carry out those parts of the liturgy for which they are responsible.

2:45 p.m. Concretizing

Staff: one person

Purposes: to remind the retreatants of the purposes of the retreat and to challenge them to keep alive any commitments or resolutions made during the retreat

Materials needed: a Bible

Description of activities

"Take a moment and reflect on how you are feeling now. You have experienced various ways to pray. I encourage you and challenge you to make the time and effort to grow in an intimate relationship with the Lord. It takes effort, as does any significant relationship. No one can do it for you. Include Scripture in your prayer on a regular basis. Remember what Saint Paul said to the Romans. [Read Rom. 8:24–27.] We will continue to pray for you. I encourage you to do the same for one another. Now, I invite you to go to one another and offer a sign of thanks."

3:00 p.m. Departure

What to Consider Before the Retreat

The introduction to this manual contains useful information about what to consider in advance of a retreat. The reader is here referred to that material, and specific additions for this retreat are also noted below.

Details in advance: See pages 11–12.

Personnel needed: See page 12.

Agenda for the staff preretreat planning meeting: See page 12.

Materials needed: See page 12.

In addition, for *liturgy preparation,* bring decoration supplies (crayons, scissors, glue, tape, construction paper, pencils, a ruler, and a large piece of butcher paper).

For the *reconciliation service,* bring a sandbox, an Easter candle, and a small candle for each retreatant.

Miscellaneous materials needed are envelopes, a Bible for each retreatant, a candle for night prayer, a slide projector, a screen, slides of nature, songbooks for the songfest, and rain gear (to be brought by the retreatants in the event it is raining during the nature walk).

The handout that follows should be reproduced in advance.

Right: Protect me, O God; I trust in you for safety.
I say to the LORD, "You are my LORD;
all the good things I have come from you."

Left: You, LORD, are all I have,
and you give me all I need;
my future is in your hands.
How wonderful are your gifts to me;
how good they are!

Right: I praise the LORD, because he guides me. . . .
I am always aware of the LORD's presence;
he is near, and nothing can shake me.

Left: And so I am thankful and glad,
and I feel completely secure,
because you protect me from the power of death. . . .
and you will not abandon me to the world of the dead.

All: You will show me the path that leads to life;
your presence fills me with joy
and brings me pleasure forever.

(Psalm 16:1-2,5-11, GNB)

Retreat 7
Parent-Teen Relationships
(Overnight Version)

Goals

The retreat "Parent-Teen Relationships (Overnight Version)" is a two-day program designed for ten to twenty-five parent-teen couples. The participants have the opportunity to enjoy the company of their related partners, as well as to get to know other parents and teens.

The goals of the retreat are the following:

1. The retreatants will examine with their peers their own experiences of parent-teen relationships.
2. The retreatants will discuss with their related partners the strengths and weaknesses of their relationship.
3. The retreatants will build the skills of communicating with their related partners.

Schedule

Day 1

9:00 a.m.	Arrival
9:30 a.m.	Introduction and prayer
10:00 a.m.	Icebreakers
10:45 a.m.	Break
11:00 a.m.	Small group 1—parent-teen partners
12:00 m.	Lunch
1:45 p.m.	Peer dyads
3:15 p.m.	Break
3:30 p.m.	Small group 2
4:45 p.m.	Break
5:00 p.m.	Liturgy preparation
6:00 p.m.	Dinner
7:00 p.m.	Strength-weakness dyads
9:00 p.m.	Reconciliation
10:30 p.m.	Closedown

Day 2

8:00 a.m.	Wake-up call
8:30 a.m.	Breakfast
9:00 a.m.	Cleanup
9:30 a.m.	Morning prayer
10:30 a.m.	Small group 3—parent-teen partners
11:05 a.m.	Letter writing
12:00 m.	Lunch
1:15 p.m.	Liturgy
2:30 p.m.	Concretizing
3:00 p.m.	Departure

Retreat Activities: Day 1

9:00 a.m. Arrival

Two staff members welcome and register the retreatants, help them locate their rooms, and have them fill out name tags.

9:30 a.m. Introduction and prayer

Staff: two people (including one to assist with the distribution of handouts)

Purposes: to lead the retreat community in prayer, to introduce the theme of the retreat, to introduce the retreat staff, and to explain guidelines for using the retreat facility

Materials needed: Handout 7–A, "Uniqueness Prayer"; a tape recorder; and an appropriate tape

Description of activities

Gather the parents and young people in the chapel, where taped music is playing as they arrive.

Part 1: "Welcome to this retreat. My name is _____. My hope is that this time you will be spending with your partner will be a very special time in your life. Let's pause a moment to ask God to bless us during these days together." Pause.

"Loving God, you have told us that when two or more are gathered in your name, you are present. We have come together in your name. We pray that you might be present to us and bless us as we come to know one another a little better. Also, watch over our family members who have remained at home so that we might have this time together. We ask that you might give to us the grace needed to work with you and our partner in an honest and trusting manner. And all of this we pray in Jesus' name. Amen.

"It is not by accident that we begin this retreat in the chapel with a prayer. I believe that it is very important to invite God to walk with us throughout this retreat. Please feel free to come into the chapel anytime throughout your stay.

"I would like to make some brief comments about retreats. By definition the word *retreat* means to step back in order to regroup. We all live in a very busy time. I have found that when I step back from my busy schedule, I am able to regroup my thoughts and energies, so that I can go forward more focused and stronger.

"We provide an environment for you and your partner to step back in order to reflect on and build upon the relationship that already exists between the two of you. I invite you to participate as best you can. Be open to risking a bit. Try to trust the staff, trust the program, and trust your partner. If you do this, I believe that when the time comes to return home, you will be thankful.

"Communication is an important part of this retreat. As you know, this is a vital ingredient for any healthy relationship. The schedule will offer you times to work on your communication skills. There will be times when we will come together as a large group for some playful and some serious activities. We will meet in small groups for discussions. But most importantly, there will be quite a bit of free time for you and your partner to relax with each other. I encourage you to spend most of the free time with your partner. It is so seldom that a parent and child can have quality time without any interruptions."

Distribute Handout 7–A. "Before I introduce the staff to you, let's join in praying the 'Uniqueness Prayer.' " Together read the prayer from the handout.

Part 2: See part 2 of the "Description of activities" on page 14 of Retreat 1 for the introductions and the practical details. At the conclusion, invite the retreatants to the location of the icebreakers.

10:00 a.m. Icebreakers

Staff: one person

Purpose: to help the retreatants feel more at ease with one another

Materials needed: Handout 7–B, "People Bingo"; a pencil for each retreatant

Description of activities

1. Introduction: "We're going to do what are called *icebreakers.* The purpose of this time together is to help us know one another a little better and to allow our playfulness to come alive."

2. Birth dates: "This first icebreaker takes a spirit of cooperation and a willingness to work together. I would like you to line up in a circle according to the date of your birth. We'll start the circle here [point to a specific spot in the room], with the person whose birth date is closest to the first of January. From here everyone will line up in a circle, ending with the person whose birth date is closest to the thirty-first of December. Are there any questions? [Pause.] Begin."

After the group has assembled in the circle, check the dates by having each person state his or her birth date.

3. Favorite musicians: "Now that was pretty easy. It didn't take too much effort. I would like you to line up in a circle again. However, this time I want you to line up alphabetically by the first letter of the name of your favorite musical artist or group. *A* lines up here and *Z* would be over here. Any questions? [Pause.] Begin."

After the group is lined up, ask the individuals or those grouped by the same artist to state their favorite musical artist or group. Encourage the others to listen and respond appropriately.

4. ''People Bingo'': "This last icebreaker will give you an opportunity to get around the room and get to know a lot of people. It is called 'People Bingo.' Each person will be given a pencil and a paper with twenty-five squares. Each square has a statement or an activity written within it.

"The object of the game is to have twenty-five different people sign your paper, each in a square that lists an activity they are able to perform or an experience they have had. You may sign your own paper only once. You may sign as many other papers as you wish. However, you may not sign any one individual's paper more than once." If your group has fewer than twenty-five members, you will have to modify the directions to allow some individuals to sign more than one square.

"The first person to have his or her paper completely signed will be the winner. [Repeat the directions.] Do you have any questions? Please bring your paper to me when you have it completely signed. . . . Begin."

When the papers are completed, have everyone sit in a circle. Take each square one at a time and ask the individuals who signed it to perform the stated activity or to say something about the experience indicated in the square. Encourage a spirit of playfulness. When the activity is completed, collect the papers and pencils.

5. Conclusion: "Thank you for your cooperation and openness to one another. I hope that you can bring that same spirit of cooperation and openness to your small group.

"I would like to divide you into small groups. We will then take a fifteen-minute break. Please gather after the break in your small group's room." Read the list of names for each small group and explain the locations of the meeting rooms.

10:45 a.m. Break

11:00 a.m. Small group 1— parent-teen partners

Staff: one person for each small group

Purposes: to invite the retreatants to introduce their partners (parent or teen) to the group and to encourage the retreatants to set a personal goal for the retreat

Materials needed for each small group: a roll of masking tape, three pieces of butcher paper, and a felt-tip marker

Description of activities
1. Introductions (25 min.): "This is the first of three times that you will meet in a small group. This first session is simply a time for introductions and goal setting. Let's begin by introducing your partner to the group. Please feel free to ask questions, as this is a time for you to get to know one another."

Have the retreatants in turn introduce their respective partners to the group. Encourage questions and responses, and make comments yourself on things of interest that you notice in the introductions.

2. Goal setting (5 min.): "Now that we know each other a little better, would someone like to start us off by telling why you came on the retreat? We won't be going around the room in a particular order. Yet, I would like for everyone to try to say something." Encourage the retreatants to talk briefly about why they joined the retreat.

"If you were to set a goal for yourself for this retreat, what would it be? What do you and your partner need at this time in your relationship? Take a few minutes to talk it over with your partner. I would then like to write the goals down. During the last small group of the retreat, we will check with you to see how you did on your goal."

While the group is thinking about the goals, list each person's name on the butcher paper. When the person explains his or her goal to the group, write it down on the paper after the name. Be sure each person states a goal.

Sometimes a parent speaks for the teenager. If this is the case, be sure to ask the teenager separately what the goal is that he or she has set.

3. Small-group guidelines (10 min.): "The next thing for us to do is to set some guidelines for our discussions in the small group. From your experience, what is it that makes a small-group discussion successful? We will list these and use them as guidelines or ground rules." Have someone list these on a piece of butcher paper. Be sure the following are included: confidentiality, honesty, trust, openness, no put-downs, an attempt to participate by all, and a willingness to speak to others in the group, not just the facilitator.

Encourage the retreatants to explain why they think a particular guideline is helpful.

4. Conclusion (5 min.): "Thank you for your cooperation. I challenge you to make choices to work toward the goal you set in this group. As you know, the retreat staff provide the environment and you do most of the work. Before we break from the group, do you have any questions about the schedule or the facilities?"

Invite a retreatant to offer a closing prayer.

12:00 m. Lunch

One staff person is available to make announcements and to choose a retreatant to lead the grace before the meal.

1:45 p.m. Peer dyads

Staff: two people (including one to assist with distributing the handouts)

Purposes: to pair each retreatant with a peer and to invite them to practice listening skills in these dyads

Materials needed: Handout 7–C, "Dyad Questions"

Description of activities
1. Background on communication: "This afternoon I am going to speak briefly about communication. Then we will assign you a partner from your peers—that is, parents will be with parents and teens with teens—and will invite you to practice communication skills.

"Listening well is an exercise in attention and hard work. Most of us do not listen well because we are not willing to do the work. Most of us have flabby muscles when it comes to listening. Only practice will strengthen these flabby muscles.

"True listening involves total concentration on the other. Temporarily, I must set myself aside. The speaker is more inclined to open up to someone who is really concentrating on him or her.

"The other side of communication is speaking. Interpersonal communication is not lecturing; lecturing often arouses indifference in a listener. Interpersonal communication is not making pronouncements; pronouncements often lead to resentment or rebellious behavior. In true communication, I communicate to share myself and to search with others.

"So, how do I begin? In his book *Between People,* John Sanford refers to communication as similar to a game of catch. In a game of catch, I start by tossing a ball so it can be caught and tossed back. Communication starts in the same 'handle gently' manner. A wild throw—such as 'You always think that'—may break up the game.

"A good communicator brings interest, attention, eye contact, trust, and feelings to an interaction. If both parties in an interaction bring those qualities, they are off to a good start."

2. Activity: "During the next hour, I invite you to practice your communication skills. You will be discussing with another person your responses to some of the 'Dyad Questions' I'll be giving you." Explain the structure of the dyad activity that is described below.
a. Person *A* listens for fifteen minutes while Person *B* speaks.
b. Person *B* listens for fifteen minutes while Person *A* speaks.
c. Persons *A* and *B* share freely for thirty minutes.

Announce the pairs of peers—parent with parent, teen with teen. Distribute Handout 7–C, the "Dyad Questions," to be used in the activity. Invite the pairs to find a quiet spot. Announce when it is time to change roles. Strongly emphasize that the listening person is not to say *anything* in response to the speaker, when in the role of the listener.

3. Closure: Invite all the retreatants to return to the room. Ask them to comment on the experiences they had in the dyads.

3:15 p.m. Break

3:30 p.m. Small group 2

Staff: one person for each small group

Purposes: to divide the retreatants into small groups *without their related partners* and to invite these unrelated parents and teens to discuss their experiences

Materials needed for each small group: four felt-tip markers and six signs on butcher paper ("Parents always . . ." "Parents never . . ." "Parents should . . ." "Teens always . . ." "Teens never . . ." "Teens should . . .")

Description of activities
1. Introduction (5 min.): "How are you doing so far? Before we begin this small group, let's take a few minutes to introduce ourselves to one another. We will go around the room. When it is your turn, simply tell us your name. I will begin. My name is . . ." Go around the circle and have the members introduce themselves.

2. Small-group guidelines (5 min.): "During the first small group, guidelines were discussed. Let's remind ourselves of these." Read the guidelines written on the butcher paper. The members of the group were probably with a different facilitator for the first small group. If this is the case, encourage them to add to the paper additional guidelines they may have.

3. Activity (15 min.): "During this time, you will have an opportunity to talk with one another about common concerns or issues that are part of parent and teen relationships. To get you thinking, I would like to first divide you into two groups. The parents will go over to this side of the room and the teens will be on the other side.

"I would like you to take about ten minutes to brainstorm with each other on this topic: What are some myths about parents and teens? Each group has three pieces of butcher paper and felt-tip markers. List as many statements as you can on the individual papers.

"Parents, you will be completing the statements *Teens always . . . Teens never . . . Teens should . . .*

"Teens, you will be completing the statements *Parents always . . . Parents never . . . Parents should . . .*

"Now, I realize that what you'll be coming up with are myths. But it will give us some things to focus on for our discussion. These can be positive or negative statements. I encourage you to be as creative as possible. Are there any questions? . . . Let's begin."

Spend time with each group to make sure they understand the instructions. Give a two-minute warning when time is almost up. Then bring the group back to the circle and hang the papers on the wall.

4. Discussion (45 min.): "I would like everyone to take a few minutes to read the statements. Choose a few statements that you would like to address. [Pause.] Let's begin with the teens. Are there any statements that you wrote or that the parents wrote that you would like to address?" Encourage the participants to talk with one another in an open and respectful manner.

5. Conclusion (5 min.): "Before we close, I would like to give everyone the opportunity to make a closing statement. Is there anything that you would like to say to the group? [Go around the circle, giving everyone the opportunity to make a statement.] Thanks again for your cooperation." Invite a retreatant to offer a closing prayer, then tell the retreatants there will be a break until time for the liturgy preparation.

4:45 p.m. Break

5:00 p.m. Liturgy preparation

See the Appendix, pages 103–107, for a full explanation of the work of the committees and instructions for presenting the session on liturgy preparation to the retreatants.

6:00 p.m. Dinner

One staff person is available to make announcements and to choose a retreatant to lead the grace.

7:00 p.m. Strength-weakness dyads

Staff: two people (including one to assist with the handouts and the tape recorder)

Purposes: to invite the retreatants to reflect on their relationships with their respective partners (parent or teen) and to provide a structure for the related parents and teens to talk with one another

Materials needed: a pencil for each retreatant; Handout 7-D, "Strength-Weakness Statements for Dyads"; a tape recorder; and an appropriate tape (e.g., "Cat's in the Cradle" by Harry Chapin)

Description of activities

1. Introduction: "Earlier today you were able to practice your communication skills with a peer. Tonight you have the opportunity to communicate with your partner. This activity can truly be a sacramental moment—a sign of God's love in your life.

"Please reflect on your relationship with your partner while I play a song that deals with the communication between a child and his parent." Play "Cat's in the Cradle" by Harry Chapin.

"In that song, neither person could make time to listen to the other. You are different, though. You have made time for your parent or teen by being on this retreat. This evening, I encourage you to give each other even more, with your gentle honesty in sharing. In approaching each other, be gentle. This dyad experience is a rare opportunity to discuss how you can better your relationship with each other. Come to each other as two treasures meeting." Explain the structure of the activity described below.

2. Activity

a. Both the parent and the teen reflect on and complete the strength-weakness statements for dyads (20 min.).

b. They exchange papers (the teen goes to the parent's room, then to another room alone) and privately read each other's answers (10 min.).

c. The teen returns to the parent's room. The teen talks while the parent listens. If the teen is uncomfortable going first, then the parent will speak first (15 min.).

d. The parent talks while the teen listens (15 min.).

e. The parent and the teen share freely with each other (30 min.).

Once the parents and the young people understand the directions for the dyads, hand out the "Strength-Weakness Statements for Dyads." Ask the parents to go to their rooms. Ask the teens to go to the dining room. Announce when it is time to go to the next step in the activity.

3. Closure: There is no special closure for this activity. The retreatants should go directly to the chapel for the reconciliation service.

9:00 p.m. Reconciliation

Staff: one leader and several priests, depending upon the number of retreatants

Purpose: to invite the retreatants to receive the Sacrament of Reconciliation

Materials needed: a small candle for each retreatant, an Easter candle, an aluminum roasting pan filled with sand, a Bible, a tape recorder, and appropriate tapes

Description of activities

The Easter candle is burning in a prominent place. The small candles are placed near the Easter candle. The aluminum pan is filled with sand and placed near the Easter candle.

1. Opening prayer: "As you spoke to each other during the strength-weakness dyad, a reconciliation process began. To reconcile is to restore or to make good again. We gather now to reconcile with God and with each other by asking forgiveness. Let us begin this reconciliation service by offering a prayer.

"God of power and mercy, open our hearts in welcome. Remove the things that hinder us from receiving one another and from receiving Christ. We hope to share in Christ's peace, mercy, and forgiveness when he comes in glory. We ask this through Christ, our Lord. Amen."

2. Seventy times seven: Read Matt. 18:21–22. "Jesus assures Peter that we must continue to forgive one another regardless of the count. As Christians we believe in forgiveness for ourselves as well as for others. We proclaim this during Sunday Mass in our Profession of Faith."

3. Examination of conscience: "I would like to read a list of questions about areas that need forgiveness. In what areas do you need forgiveness? Please reflect on your life." Read the examination of conscience below.

- Have I broken promises?
- Have I not always taken time to listen?
- Have I been distracted from my family by work, school, or friends?
- Have I let my fears stand between my loved ones and me?
- Have I held grudges and refused to forgive?
- Have I shut a loved one out of certain areas of my life?
- Have I not expressed the love I feel?
- Are there other areas of my relationships where I have failed to love and to give of myself to my loved ones?

4. Confessions: "At this time I invite each of you to be reconciled. Perhaps you wish to come to the priest with your partner and ask for forgiveness for a particular area that involves the two of you. Or you may wish to approach him alone."

Indicate the priest(s) who will be hearing confessions. If there is more than one priest available for the sacrament, tell the retreatants where each will be located. Explain that they have the option of going to confession for the Sacrament of Reconciliation, of simply asking the priest for a blessing, or of asking him to pray with them for a particular concern.

"After seeing Father, come to the Easter candle. This is the Christ candle, which is blessed during the Easter Vigil Mass. The flame is a sign of the presence of God. God's love is always being offered to us. As a sign of having been reconciled, take a mini–Christ candle. Light the small candle and place it in the box of sand. Your light will shine for all the world to see." Dim the lights and play soft music.

5. Closing: As a closing, gather all in a circle. Join hands and pray the Lord's Prayer.

10:30 p.m. Closedown

One staff person announces the schedule for the next day and other information.

Retreat Activities: Day 2

8:00 a.m. Wake-up call

8:30 a.m. Breakfast

9:00 a.m. Cleanup

Staff: one person

Purpose: to instruct the retreatants on the expectations for preparing for departure and to provide time for them to change sheets, clean rooms, pack, and load the cars or the bus

Materials: none

9:30 a.m. Morning prayer

Staff: two people (including one to assist with the handouts)

Purposes: to invite the retreatants to reflect upon their relationship with God and to encourage the retreatants to discuss their experience of God with their respective partners (parent or teen)

Materials: Handout 7–E, "God in My Life"; a Bible

Description of activities

"Good morning! Let's begin our day by taking time to place ourselves in the presence of God. [Pause.] During this retreat many of the activities have dealt with communication. Yesterday, you had the opportunity to practice communication skills in dyads. At one time this was with a peer, and then last night you spoke with your partner.

"Our prayer this morning is a continuation of this type of communication. The topic is 'God in my life.' I would like to give you the opportunity to reflect on the times you have felt God's presence in your life. What were the circumstances? Who were the people who influenced your understanding of God? What were significant experiences that may have influenced your understanding of God? What does your relationship with God mean to you today?"

The presenter offers examples of his or her experience with prayer, such as the following two. "My mom and dad were very influential in my understanding of God. We often prayed together as a family. When I was a young child, Mom and Dad said my night prayers with me. I grew up being taught that prayer ought to be a part of my daily schedule.

"A second example in my experience is concerned with the beauty of nature. I was out for a walk this morning and couldn't help noticing the beauty of creation. Often, I find it so easy to experience the peacefulness and creativity of our God when I take the time to be still among the simple things of life.

"Those are two examples from my experience. What is your experience? To help you reflect, I would like to read Ps. 139." Very slowly read Ps. 139:1–18,23–34. Remain still for a short time after reading the psalm.

"The next thirty minutes have been set aside for you and your partner to continue this prayer together. I encourage you to talk with each other about your experience of God. As an aid, I will give you some questions about the topic 'God in my life.' By no means do you need to stick with the questions on the paper. If something comes up that you feel is more important to talk about, then by all means do so.

"After the thirty minutes are up, we will gather in our small groups—the first group you met in. Please note the group to which you belong and the room in which you will be meeting. I invite you to remain in the chapel or go out for a walk as you spend the next thirty minutes with your partner. Does anyone have any questions?" Distribute Handout 7–E, "God in My Life."

10:30 a.m. Small group 3— parent-teen partners

Staff: one person for each small group

Purposes: to summarize the retreat for the participants and to introduce the letter writing

Materials needed for each small group: a piece of stationery, a pencil, and an envelope for each retreatant; Handout 7–F, "Letter Questions"

Description of activities

1. Introduction (20 min.): "During this group activity we'll be talking about your experience of the retreat. Let's take a look at the goals that you set for yourselves during the first small group. [Pause.] How did you do on your goal? Was there any activity that helped you to reach your goal? We can go in any order. However, I would like to hear from everyone." Encourage all members to comment on how they did on their retreat goals. This discussion does not need to be structured. Invite the retreatants to respond to one another.

2. Closing comments (5 min.): "Is there any comment that you would like to make to the group?" Give everyone a chance to make a comment.

3. Introduction to letter writing (10 min.): "We have spent a brief time together in this group summarizing your experience of the retreat. To assist you in bringing things to a close with your partner, we have set aside the time until lunch for you to write a letter. This will give you a way to express in writing what the retreat experience with your partner has meant to you."

Distribute Handout 7–F. "To assist you, I am giving you some questions on a handout. Find a quiet place where you can be alone. Reflect on the questions. Perhaps there is something else on your mind. Are there any commitments that you would like to make to your partner? After thinking about this, write the letter to your partner. Seal the letter in the envelope provided. Please write your partner's first and last name on the envelope. These letters will then be exchanged during the liturgy. Are there any questions? . . . When you have finished, please place your pencil, the question sheet, and the sealed letter in the boxes provided. [Name the location of the boxes.] You have until lunch to write your letters."

11:05 a.m. Letter writing

12:00 m. Lunch

One staff person is available to make announcements and to choose a retreatant to lead the grace before the meal.

1:15 p.m. Liturgy

The committees carry out those parts of the liturgy for which they are responsible.

The letters that were written after the third small group are placed upon the altar. Following the homily, invite the teens to come up and pick up both their parents' letters and their own letters. Ask them to bring the letters back to where they were sitting and exchange them with their parents. Allow ten to fifteen minutes for reading the letters. Soft instrumental music can be played in the background.

2:30 p.m. Concretizing

Staff: one person

Purposes: to remind the retreatants of the retreat theme and to challenge them to keep alive any commitments or resolutions made during the retreat

Materials needed: none

Description of activities

"Please take a moment to be aware of your feelings. [Pause.] You are the person responsible for these feelings. I imagine most of you feel pretty good about this experience. I challenge you to take home with you what you have practiced here. Take home with you a spirit of prayerfulness, a spirit of reconciliation, honesty, attentive listening, playfulness, and love. You have truly gifted one another. Continue to give to your partner and to each of your family members.

"The letters you shared certainly are love letters. Cherish them. Refer to them often and think of this time together. We will pray for you and for your families. Please take time to pray for one another.

"Before we end the retreat, let's offer each other a sign of thanks."

3:00 p.m. Departure

What to Consider Before the Retreat

The introduction to this manual contains useful information about what to consider in advance of a retreat. The reader is here referred to that material, and specific additions for this retreat are also noted below.

Details in advance: See pages 11–12.

Personnel needed: See page 12.

Agenda for the staff preretreat planning meeting: See page 12. For the division of the retreatants into small groups, note that groups 1 and 3 on the schedule have the same composition, that is, parent and son or daughter are together. Small group 2, however, is composed of parents and teens who are unrelated to one another. The small groups should have a balance of men and women, and if possible, the teens should be divided by grade (e.g., ninth graders in different groups from twelfth graders).

Materials needed: See page 12.

In addition, for *liturgy preparation,* bring decoration supplies (crayons, scissors, glue, tape, construction paper, pencils, a ruler, and a large piece of butcher paper) and five Bibles.

For the *reconciliation service,* bring a small candle for each retreatant, an Easter candle, and an aluminum roasting pan filled with sand.

Miscellaneous materials needed are an envelope for each retreatant and six signs on butcher paper ("Parents always . . ." "Parents never . . ." "Parents should . . ." "Teens always . . ." "Teens never . . ." "Teens should . . .")

The handouts that follow should be reproduced in advance, with each handout on its own page.

Uniqueness Prayer

Left: I am unique, Lord, for I am the expression of your love, and no two moments of love are ever the same. Each is separate, intimately personal. Each is an original reflection of your own love-laden personality.

Right: And because I am unique, Lord, I have a unique contribution to make to your love-mission on earth.

Left: There are people whom only I can love in the way that counts . . . people waiting for my touch, eyes searching for my look of understanding, hands reaching for my extended strength, arms waiting for my embrace.

Right: Lord, what mystery and magnificence! That you should take my unique weakness and use it as a means of communicating your unique power; that you should select one who needs to be saved and use me to save others.

All: Empower me, Lord. Cast out shadows so that only beauty and brightness go forth from the unique me to another you.

(Written by Andre Auw)

Directions: In the exercise below there are twenty-five squares, each containing a statement or an activity. The object is to find a person within the group who has had one of the experiences listed, or who is able to perform one of the activities.

You may sign your own "bingo card" only once. You may sign as many other papers as you wish, but you may not sign any one individual's more than once.

The first person to completely fill his or her card is the winner.

1	2	3	4	5
Knows who Boy George is	Voted in the Johnson versus Goldwater election	Knows who barks at the moon	Knows a "dead head"	Once had a crew cut
6 Knows who Joe McCarthy was	**7** Can speak more than one language	**8** Has celebrated a twenty-fifth anniversary	**9** Knows a clean, funny joke	**10** Can name five characters from *The Howdy Doody Show*
11 Watched the Beatles on *The Ed Sullivan Show*	**12** Has lettered in a varsity sport lately	★ Knows what "poppin" is	**14** Has or had a paper route	**15** Wears contact lenses
16 Knows the real names of the stars of *From Here to Eternity*	**17** Can name three people who have been on *Saturday Night Live*	**18** Has been to a prom in the past year	**19** Wears or wore a miniskirt	**20** Has been to a rock concert lately
21 Has used hacky sac	**22** Liked Fabian	**23** Knows who the B-52s are	**24** Knows who Nina Blackwood is	**25** Has played with a hula hoop

Directions: The object of the exercise below is to sharpen communication skills. Partners will take turns asking questions and listening to the responses of each other according to the directions that follow.

- Person *A* asks questions and listens to the response of person *B* (15 min.).
- Then the roles are exchanged, and person *B* asks questions and listens to the responses of person *A* (15 min.). Note: When taking the role of listener, nothing may be said in response to the speaker.
- Finally, persons *A* and *B* freely discuss the questions and responses they shared previously (30 min.).

1. What are the fondest memories you have of your parent (teen)?

2. In twenty years, what will be your parent's (teen's) memory of you?

3. What can you do that will produce better memories for your parent (teen)?

4. What types of things are you not willing to hear from your parent (teen)?

5. How are family decisions and policies reached in your home?

6. What makes it easy for you to listen to your parent (teen)?

7. How do you feel when you sense that your parent (teen) has really listened to you?

8. How could you become a better listener?

9. When have you felt most distant from your parent (teen)?

10. When have you felt closest to your parent (teen)?

11. What personal characteristics do you and your parent (teen) have that are similar?

12. When do you feel the most needed by your parent (teen)?

13. What do you add to your parent's (teen's) life?

14. In what way do you show your parent (teen) that you love him or her?

15. What feelings are difficult for you to express to your parent (teen)?

Directions for parent-teen dyads

1. Reflect on the statements in the exercise below and then complete each one (20 min.).
2. Exchange papers with your partner and privately read the answers (10 min.).
3. Meet with your partner and take turns speaking and listening to the responses (15 min. for each person).
4. Finally, freely share your responses with each other (30 min.).

1. I think my strong points are . . .

2. I think your strong points are . . .

3. I think my weak points are . . .

4. I think your weak points are . . .

5. One of my greatest fears is . . .

6. I think one of your greatest fears is . . .

7. I think one of the best things I have done for you is . . .

8. I think one of the best things you have done for me is . . .

9. I think one of my biggest achievements was . . .

10. I think one of your biggest achievements was . . .

11. I think one of the hard things about being your parent (teen) is . . .

12. I think one of the best things about being your parent (teen) is . . .

Directions: The following list of questions is intended to help you and your partner to reflect and discuss with each other your experiences of God. Please feel free to add other questions and discuss them (30 min.). Space has been provided if you wish to make notes on your answers.

1. Who taught you about God?

2. What were you taught?

3. How would you describe God?

4. How do you get in touch with God?

5. How do you pray?

6. How does God contact you?

7. What is the best part of your relationship with God?

8. What is the most difficult part of your relationship with God?

9. When do you pray?

10. Where are you and God in relationship right now?

Directions: Before you begin this activity, find a quiet place where you can be alone to reflect on the questions printed below.

Using the spaces provided, make a few notes about your reflections. Think about any commitments that you might want to make to your retreat partner. Then, on the stationery, write a letter to him or her explaining these thoughts and feelings.

Seal your letter in the envelope provided and write your partner's first and last name on the front.

• What activities, events, or people made an impression on you during this retreat?

• What did you learn or relearn about yourself, others, your parent (teen), and God during this retreat?

• How do you feel about your relationship with your parent (teen) at this moment? How has it changed as a result of spending time together during this retreat?

• What would you like to say to your parent (teen) that still is left unsaid?

• What do you plan to do about what you have learned? Be specific and practical.

• Describe some specific ways in which you plan to affirm the uniqueness of your parent (teen), for example, by listening, trusting, confronting, or spending more time together.

Part C
Weekend Retreats

Retreat 8 ("Journey") is designed for older (eleventh- and twelfth-grade) retreatants. The participants reflect on the process of growth that has taken place in their relationships with family members, friends, self, and God, and they examine ways to follow Jesus more closely. This retreat can be used as a mandatory program.

Retreat 9 ("Parent-Teen Relationships") is for pairs that consist of a teenaged retreatant with a parent. The pair could be a daughter-mother, daughter-father, son-mother, or son-father couple. The teen and parent couple have the opportunity to spend time together in playful, prayerful, relaxed, and serious activities. This program is an expanded version of Retreat 7. It is offered in a weekend as well as an overnight format because the value of this program cannot be overstated.

Retreat 10 ("Peacemakers") is designed for any teenaged retreatant. The participants examine their attitudes toward being peacemakers, and they reflect on ways to integrate peaceful actions into their own lives. It is important that the retreatants have freely chosen to attend this program.

Retreat 8
Journey

Goals

The retreat "Journey" has been designed for older (eleventh- and twelfth-grade) retreatants. It is a three-day program—Friday evening to Sunday afternoon—for twenty-five to forty-five participants.

The goals of the retreat are the following:
1. The retreatants will examine their relationships with family, friends, self, and God, using Jesus as a model.
2. The retreatants will examine ways in which they trust and listen in their current relationships.
3. The retreatants will experience various types of communal prayer.

Schedule

Day 1

7:00 p.m.	Arrival
7:30 p.m.	Introduction and prayer
8:15 p.m.	Icebreakers
9:00 p.m.	Small group 1
10:00 p.m.	Break
10:30 p.m.	Night prayer
11:00 p.m.	Closedown

Day 2

7:45 a.m.	Wake-up call
8:00 a.m.	Breakfast
8:45 a.m.	Morning prayer
9:15 a.m.	"Trust walk"
10:30 a.m.	Break
10:45 a.m.	Small group 2
12:00 m.	Lunch
12:45 p.m.	Organized recreation
2:30 p.m.	Quiet time
3:00 p.m.	Dyads
4:15 p.m.	Break
4:30 p.m.	Small group 3
6:00 p.m.	Dinner
7:15 p.m.	Reconciliation
8:45 p.m.	Break
9:30 p.m.	Liturgy preparation
10:30 p.m.	Break
10:45 p.m.	Night prayer
11:15 p.m.	Closedown

Day 3

7:45 a.m.	Wake-up call
8:00 a.m.	Breakfast
8:45 a.m.	Cleanup
9:30 a.m.	Morning prayer
10:15 a.m.	Break
10:30 a.m.	Small group 4
12:15 p.m.	Lunch
1:15 p.m.	Liturgy
2:30 p.m.	Concretizing
3:00 p.m.	Departure

Retreat Activities: Day 1

7:00 p.m. Arrival

Two staff members welcome and register the retreatants, help them locate their rooms, and have them fill out name tags.

7:30 p.m. Introduction and prayer

Staff: two people (including one to assist with the tape recorder)

Purposes: to lead the retreat community in prayer, to introduce the theme of the retreat, to introduce the retreat staff, and to explain guidelines for using the retreat facility

Materials needed: a tape recorder and a tape of an appropriate song (e.g., the theme song from *Mahogany,* "Do You Know Where You Are Going To?")

Description of activities

Part 1: "I would like to welcome you to this retreat. My name is _____. As we begin our retreat, let us remember that we are in the holy presence of God. [Pause.] Lord, we place our lives in your presence. We ask your blessing on us as we step aside from our busy lives in order to look at our relationships with you and others. Please be with us to help and guide us so that we might come to love as Jesus has taught. We pray this in Jesus' name. Amen.

"The theme for this retreat is 'Journey.' This weekend, you will have the opportunity to reflect on your relationships with yourself, God, your family, and your friends. Where have you been in these relationships? Where are you now? Where would you like to be in the future?

"Regarding yourself—how do you see yourself? Do you accept yourself and accept how rare the treasure is that you are? Or do you give yourself messages that you are not worthy of love?

"Regarding God—where are you and God in relationship today? Is there a relationship at all? Where would you like to be in your relationship with God in the future?

"Regarding your family members—what are the differences in how you related to them in the past and how you relate to them now? What are the areas of support within your family? What are the areas of tension?

"Regarding your friends—what do your friends mean to you today? Where would you like to be with them in the future? Do you need to reconcile with anyone? Do you need to offer thanks or support to any of your friends?

"These are all questions that you will have time to examine during the retreat. There will also be times when you will come together in playfulness, as well as in seriousness. We will have four different opportunities to meet in small groups in order to talk about what our personal experiences have been.

"For you to get the most out of these days together, I encourage you to take responsibility for your actions. Trust the staff as well as one another. Risk a bit in allowing others to know you and in getting to know one another. Try your best to drop any stereotypes you may have. They keep you from being open to the uniqueness and specialness of others. If you come with an openness and a real effort to participate in each activity, you will be pleased with how you feel by the end of the retreat.

"Take a few minutes to reflect in silence on a goal that you would like to set for yourself for these retreat days. What do you need now in your life? What are the relational areas that need to be explored in your life?

"There will be some music in the background while you have this time to reflect on your goal for the retreat." Play the theme song from *Mahogany,* "Do You Know Where You Are Going To?"

"Quietly offer a personal prayer asking God to assist you in working toward your goal." Pause.

Part 2: See part 2 of the "Description of activities" on page 14 of Retreat 1 for the introductions and the practical details. At the conclusion, invite the retreatants to the location of the icebreakers.

8:15 p.m. Icebreakers

Staff: one person leading, with all staff participating

Purposes: to help the retreatants feel more at ease with one another and feel a sense of cooperation, playfulness, and openness

Materials needed: Handout 8–A, "People Bingo"; "People Bingo" materials (a kazoo, a hula hoop, a jump rope, and three tennis balls for juggling); a pencil for each retreatant

Description of activities

1. Introduction: "We're about to do what are called *icebreakers.* The purpose of this time together is to help us get to know one another a little better, to let go of some stereotypes that we might have of others, and to allow our playfulness to come alive."

2. "Group Whoosh": "Let's begin. Would everyone please stand in a circle. [Pause until the circle is formed.] I know that many of you have had a long week. We need to get rid of all the stressful and anxious feelings inside us that are waiting to be released before we can get into this retreat. So I have planned for us to do the 'Group Whoosh'!

"Begin by joining hands with the persons next to you. Now raise your hands. When I count to three, everyone throw your hands down and let out a yell of "whoosh" that will release the stress and the anxiety. One, two, three . . ." Often the first try is halfhearted because most of the retreatants are self-conscious. Try it a second time if this is the case.

3. "People Bingo": Distribute Handout 8–A and the pencils. "The next icebreaker takes a spirit of cooperation and a willingness to work together. This spirit is something that will be helpful throughout the retreat and not just during the icebreakers. We are going to play 'People Bingo.' Each person will be given a pencil and a paper with twenty-five squares. Each square has a statement or an activity written within it.

"The object of this game is to have twenty-five different people sign your paper, each in a square that lists an activity that they are able to perform. You may sign your own name only once. You may sign as many other papers as you wish. However, you may not sign any one individual's paper more than once." If your group has fewer than twenty-five members, you will have to modify the directions to allow some individuals to sign more than one square.

"The first person to have his or her paper completely signed will be the winner. I will check to see if the people who signed your paper can actually do what it was that they signed. [Repeat the directions.] Please bring me your paper when it is completely signed. I will dim the lights when we have a winner. Are there any other questions? . . . Now, begin!"

When the papers are completed, have everyone sit in the circle. Take each square one at a time and ask the individual who signed it to perform the stated activity. Keep a spirit of playfulness and encourage reactions from the group. When the activity is completed, collect the papers and pencils.

4. Conclusion: "Thank you for your cooperation and your openness to one another. Soon we will be going to our small-group rooms. I hope that you can bring that same spirit of cooperation and openness to your small group.

"I would like to divide you into small groups. We will then take a ten-minute break. Please then go directly to your small group's meeting room." Read the list of names for each small group and explain the location of the meeting rooms.

9:00 p.m. Small group 1

Staff: one person for each small group

Purposes: to create an environment where the retreatants feel comfortable sharing their thoughts and feelings, to have them introduce themselves, and to have them set a goal to be worked toward during the retreat

Materials needed for each small group: two large pieces of butcher paper, a felt-tip marker, and masking tape

Description of activities

1. Introductions (20 min.): "Let's begin by getting to know a little bit about one another. Please turn to the person next to you and talk with him or her for a few minutes. Ask questions such as these: (1) What is your name and why were you named that particular name? (2) How many people are in your family and where are you in the order of births? (3) What is your favorite hobby? (4) What is a hope you have for the future? After you have gotten to know each other, then you will introduce your partner to the group." Allow five minutes for the pairs to get to know each other. Then invite them to introduce their partners. Others may respond by asking clarifying questions.

2. Guidelines (5 min.): "During this retreat we will meet as a small group four times. These discussions are meant to be a time for you to share your experiences and to hear about others' experiences. Let's establish some guidelines to be used during the discussions. I will write down the ones you suggest and hang them on the wall so that we can refer to them whenever necessary." Write the guidelines on the butcher paper. Make sure the following are included: confidentiality, respect, no put-downs, honesty, and an attempt to participate by all.

3. Goals (10 min.): Encourage the retreatants to set a retreat goal for themselves. Write these on the butcher paper and hang them in the room.

4. Discussion (20 min.): Encourage the retreatants to participate in a discussion about "yourself," using any of the questions suggested below. Make sure the guidelines are observed.
• What would you most like to do or be?
• Who do you emulate or want to be like?
• What do you fear the most?
• What are your strengths? How do you use them?
• What are your limitations? How do you deal with them?
• What things make your life complicated?
• How do you want people to remember you?

5. Summary (5 min.): "Thank you for trusting one another. I encourage you to continue to do so throughout the retreat. Remember the importance of confidentiality. Anything spoken in the group remains among us. Before we close, would anyone like to make a comment?" Give everyone a chance to make a closing statement.

6. Closure: Invite a retreatant to offer a closing prayer. Explain the schedule for the rest of the evening.

10:00 p.m. Break

10:30 p.m. Night prayer

Staff: two people (including one to assist with the tape recorder and the lights)

Purposes: to introduce the retreatants to the importance of communal prayer and to provide the opportunity for them to voice their hopes for the retreat in the form of a personal prayer

Materials needed: a candle, a tape recorder, a tape with an appropriate song (e.g., "Lord, Is It Mine?" by Supertramp), a lamp (needed if the lighting in the chapel cannot be dimmed), and a Bible

Description of activities

Have a candle lit and placed in front of the leader. "Tonight we gather to pray, with the theme of 'hope' as our focus. This evening in your small group, each of you set a goal for yourself for this retreat. This night prayer time is a chance for you to ask God to help you with your particular goal. In Scripture, we read that the Lord offers each of us a future full of hope. [Read Jer. 29:11–15 and pause for reflection.] Think about the prayer that you would like to offer while I play a song." Play "Lord, Is It Mine?" by Supertramp.

"There is a simple structure for this communal prayer. I will pass a candle around the circle. I invite each of you to offer your prayer out loud when the candle comes to you. The prayer could be one of hope for the retreat or for any other concerns of yours. If you do not wish to offer a prayer out loud, when the candle comes to you, offer a silent prayer. Please join one another in prayer by listening attentively. Seriously consider offering a prayer aloud so that we can join you in your prayer." Begin by offering a prayer of hope—"Lord, I hope . . ." —then pass the candle.

Close by reading Ps. 31:15–17,24–25.

11:00 p.m. Closedown

One staff person explains the second day's schedule and makes other announcements.

Retreat Activities: Day 2

7:45 a.m. Wake-up call

8:00 a.m. Breakfast

8:45 a.m. Morning prayer

Staff: two people (one to assist)

Purposes: to provide the retreatants with quiet time to notice the beauty of nature and with the opportunity to voice their prayers of praise

Materials needed: a Bible and volume 2 of the *Glory and Praise* songbooks

Description of activities

"Good morning! As we begin our day, let's take a moment to remember that we are in the holy presence of God." Pause.

"You might have picked up already on this retreat how important prayer is to us. We gathered in the chapel to begin the retreat. Last night before retiring, we came together for a night prayer. And now this morning we are again taking time to call upon the Lord to be present to us.

"Usually, when people pray they have one of four reasons for doing so. Perhaps the most popular type of prayer is the asking kind: 'Lord, help me to pass this exam.' A second type of prayer is one of thanks: 'Thank you, Lord, for letting him be my friend.' The third type is the kind that asks God for forgiveness. We do this during the penitential rite at Mass. The fourth type of prayer is one that I don't hear very often. This is a prayer of praise. I have chosen this type of prayer for our gathering this morning."

Offer a brief experience of nature, such as the following one. "While I was out for a walk this morning, I was very aware of the many colors and the various types of trees around the property here. Buds on the trees were numerous; birds were singing; the sky was so blue. Seeing the beauty of creation often causes me to praise the Creator.

"I would like to share the beauty of creation with you for a morning prayer. First I will read a prayer called 'The Canticle of Praise.' This is taken from the Book of Daniel." Slowly read from Dan. 3:52,57,59–60,62–68,71–76,80, 85–86,89–90.

"You will have the chance to create your own prayer of praise similar to the one found in Scripture. In a moment I will ask you to go outside. In silence, let your eyes and ears take in as much of creation as possible. Take a look at what is outside praising God. [Mention some aspects of nature's beauty that are apparent, such as the following.] Notice the sky, the cloud formations, the dew on the grass, the new growth. Listen to the sounds of the birds. Notice as much of creation as you can.

"I remind you that this is to be a time of silence. Please remain by yourself. Let it be a time of prayer. After ten minutes, please return to the chapel. Keep in mind something from nature that is particularly special to you. When you return to the chapel, we will create our own prayer of praise."

Allow ten minutes for the retreatants to quietly walk around the property. This may need to be supervised by the staff if the group is less mature.

"Here is how we will create our own prayer. I will teach you the refrain to a song. We will sing the refrain, then three people will offer their prayers of praise: 'I praise you, Lord, for . . . (say whatever it is that you saw).' After three people have said their prayers, we will sing the refrain again, then three more will offer their prayers, and so on. Since this is our prayer, I encourage everyone to sing."

Teach the refrain to the song "We Praise You," number 154 in volume 2 of the *Glory and Praise* songbook. As leader, offer the first prayer to model for the retreatants what it is you are asking them to do, for example: "I praise you, Lord, for the warmth of the sun." Be sure to allow enough time for the retreatants to offer their prayers. Sometimes it takes a while for the group to begin. Have a staff member available to offer a second prayer if necessary. Finish the prayer by having an individual sing the first verse, then have the group sing the refrain twice. (If a musician is not available, use the tape of "We Praise You" from *Glory and Praise* to teach the song.)

"Thank you for helping create our prayer. We would like to begin the next activity shortly." Give the location and time for the retreatants to gather for the "trust walk."

9:15 a.m. "Trust walk"

Staff: two people (If there is an uneven number of retreatants, an additional adult is needed.) The first staff person introduces the activity, divides the group in half, instructs the leaders about their role, and closes the activity. The second staff person instructs the followers about their role, passes out the blindfolds, and assists in any manner needed.

Purposes: to challenge the retreatants to trust another person, to encourage them to be aware of their thoughts and feelings when in a trusting relationship, and to provide them the opportunity to be trusted by another person

Materials needed: a blindfold for each retreatant and food (orange sections, apple slices, etc.)

Description of activities

1. Introduction: "I would like to speak briefly about trust in relationships. Trust is an important part of this retreat. If you were not trusting of those in your small group, then very little was said in your group last night. Trust is a key ingredient in any significant relationship.

"This morning I invite each of you to examine your ability to trust—yourself, others, and God. In a few minutes you will experience a 'trust walk.' The key to this activity is that you be aware of what is happening inside you when you are not in control and must trust another. You will have the opportunity to be both the leader and the blindfolded follower. Another important part of this activity is that it takes place in silence. I will divide you now, and half of you will receive instructions for being a leader while the other half receives instructions for being a blindfolded follower."

Divide the group in half, with the boys and the girls distributed evenly between the two groups. Try to arrange for a boy always to be paired with a girl in this activity. A boy-leading-boy arrangement takes more trust. Send the followers to another room with the assistant, who will explain the instructions. The leaders remain to receive instructions.

2. Instructions for leaders: "For the next ten minutes you will be the 'teacher.' You are the person responsible for the well-being of another. Your job is to help your partner experience as many senses as possible. Be creative. Have the person sift dirt, feel the bark of a tree, smell the flowers, taste some food. All communication is to be done in silence. Help your partner to know when to take a step by touching the person's leg. Hold your partner in a way in which both of you are comfortable. I suggest one hand on the left shoulder and the other hand on the right arm. Walk alongside so you can see for the person. Allow your partner's hands to be free to explore the environment.

"It is important that you choose as a partner someone who does not know you. Boys are to choose a girl. Girls, please choose a boy. After ten minutes, I will make an announcement. At that time bring your partner back to this room and be seated in front of him or her. I will ask a series of questions for the follower to answer. You are to remain silent throughout this question period. Does anyone have any questions?" [Pause.] Send the leaders to the other room a few at a time to choose a follower.

3. Instructions for followers: Pass out the blindfolds and take away any eyeglasses. "Please put on your blindfolds. Try to get used to wearing them. Soon the leaders will come to take you on a ten-minute walk. You won't know who your leader is. Neither of you is to communicate by speaking. Be aware of your leader's nonverbal messages. For example, touching your leg might mean to take a step. Be aware of what is going on inside you. How comfortable are you in allowing another person in your space? How do your senses come alive? . . . touch, taste, smell, hearing?

"Remember, this is a 'trust walk.' It is not something in which you judge one another but instead an opportunity to know yourself a little better. How much can you trust? How much can you allow another to lead and teach you? How do you handle your frustration and fear? Each of these questions will come up. Be silent and explore what's happening inside. Are there any questions? Please leave the blindfolds on until you are told to remove them."

4. The walk: Allow ten minutes for the "trust walk."

5. Roundup: After the walk, bring the group into the room. Ask the leaders to position themselves in front of their respective followers. Ask the questions suggested below of the followers. The leaders are to remain silent.

- What senses came alive?
- What was the most fun?
- What was the most difficult?
- How did you feel when you were waiting to be chosen?
- What did you learn about your ability to trust?
- What did you learn about your leader?
- Who do you think your leader is? Name the person you believe to be your leader, then remove your blindfold.

After the roundup, have the leaders and the followers exchange roles, with the new followers wearing the blindfolds. Bring the followers to the other room for their instructions. Remain with the new leaders to explain their instructions, then have them choose new partners from the followers. Begin the ten-minute walk again and follow with the roundup.

6. Closure: Bring the whole group together and ask the retreatants to talk about their experiences as leaders and followers. Remind them to continue to look inside to discover new insights about themselves in the area of trust.

10:30 a.m. Break

10:45 a.m. Small group 2

Staff: one person for each small group

Purpose: to create a safe atmosphere for the retreatants to explore their journeys in their relationships with God and to provide them with the opportunity to hear about one another's faith journeys

Materials needed: none

Description of activities

1. Introduction (20 min.): Invite the retreatants to talk about the night prayer of hope, the morning prayer of praise, and the "trust walk." Ask them to review their goals and the guidelines that are posted on the wall of the small group's room.

2. Discussion (50 min.): Encourage all to participate in a discussion of the topic "God," using the questions suggested below. Remind the retreatants of the guidelines, if necessary.

- What are your feelings about discussing your experience of a relationship with God?
- How would you explain God to a five-year-old child?
- How would you explain God to an eighty-year-old person?
- What did you like about what you were taught regarding God?
- What do you still question regarding what you were taught about God?
- Is a relationship with God important to you?
- What is hard about having a relationship with God?
- What is easy about having a relationship with God?
- When have you felt close to God?
- When have you felt distant from God?
- In the future, what are your hopes for your relationship with God?

3. Summary (5 min.): Encourage the retreatants to continue to question, explore, and trust. This leads to a depth of understanding and continued growth. Invite them to make closing comments.

4. Closure: Invite a retreatant to lead the group in a closing prayer.

12:00 m. Lunch

One staff person is available to make announcements and to choose a retreatant to lead the grace before the meal.

12:45 p.m. Organized recreation

Staff: two people

Purposes: to provide an opportunity for the retreatants to exercise and to encourage them to interact with one another in an active yet noncompetitive manner

Materials needed: volleyballs, Frisbees, or other equipment

2:30 p.m. Quiet time

Staff: two people (including one to assist with supervising)

Purposes: to introduce the retreatants to the value of taking some time for quiet and to invite them to reflect on their retreat goals

Materials needed: a tape recorder and a tape with appropriate music

Description of activities

"At this time in the retreat, we gather to quiet ourselves. We have just come from a time of recreation. During the next twenty minutes I invite you to find a quiet place where you can be alone. Sit down and be still. Relax your body by taking some deep breaths.

"We still have twenty-four hours of retreat left. Reflect on how you are doing on your goal. What more do you need to do in order to achieve your goal? The theme has been 'Journey.' Where have you been in your relationships? Where are you now? Where would you like to go in your relationships with family, friends, self, and God?

"If being still for twenty minutes is difficult for you, please respect the efforts of others." Explain the locations for this activity and invite the retreatants to go to a quiet spot. Turn on quiet music for those who choose to remain in the meeting room. The leader and the assistant should be available to supervise them during this activity.

3:00 p.m. Dyads

Staff: two persons (If there is an uneven number of retreatants, an additional adult is needed.)

Purpose: to provide the retreatants with the opportunity to work on listening skills

Materials needed: Handout 8–B, "Dyad Questions"; a large piece of butcher paper; and a felt-tip marker

Description of activities

1. Background on communication: "This afternoon I am going to speak briefly about communication. Then we will assign you a partner and invite you to practice some communication skills. This is probably the most difficult activity of the retreat because it asks a lot of you. Yet, it is one of the most rewarding activities, if you are able to trust yourself and your partner.

"The key to any relationship is communication. This entails both listening and being willing to share of ourselves. Listening well is an exercise in attention and hard work. Most of us do not listen well because we are not willing to do the work. Most of us have flabby muscles when it comes to listening. Only practice will strengthen these flabby muscles.

"True listening involves total concentration on the other. Temporarily, I must set myself aside. The speaker is more inclined to open up to someone who is really concentrating on him or her.

"The other side of communication is speaking. Interpersonal communication is not lecturing; lecturing often arouses indifference in a listener. Interpersonal communication is not making pronouncements; pronouncements often lead to resentment or rebellious behavior. In true communication, I communicate to share myself and to search with others.

"So, how do I begin? In his book *Between People,* John Sanford refers to communication as similar to a game of catch. In a game of catch, I start by tossing a ball so it can be caught and tossed back. Communication starts in the same 'handle gently' manner. A wild throw—such as 'You always think that'—may break up the game.

"A good communicator brings interest, attention, eye contact, trust, and feelings to an interaction. If both parties in an interaction bring these qualities, they are off to a good start. Think about a phone call. When we're on the phone most of us have our attention focused on one person. We remove all other distractions. If the phone is answered in a busy kitchen, we make sure we can find another room in which to talk."

2. Activity: "This exercise in communication takes work from you and your partner. Each of you will have the opportunity to be the speaker and the listener. The important thing to keep in mind if you are the listener is that you may not speak in response to what the speaker says. Your eye contact and nonverbal communication will let the speaker know you are interested. Your dyad partner will be the person who was your partner the first time we did the 'trust walk' this morning. If you need some help in knowing what to talk about, I will give you a list of 'Dyad Questions.' I encourage you to talk about any question that is of interest to you. Also, if you find yourself sitting in silence, try to be comfortable with that. Now I will explain how we will do the activity." Write on the butcher paper the procedure for the dyad activity described below and explain it.

a. Person *A* listens for ten minutes while Person *B* speaks.

b. Person *B* listens for ten minutes while Person *A* speaks.

c. Persons *A* and *B* share freely for twenty minutes.

Tell the retreatants that Person *A* is the leader from the first "trust walk," and Person *B* is the follower from the first "trust walk." Distribute Handout 8–B, and invite the retreatants to find a quiet place to be alone with their partners. The leader and the assistant should be available to supervise.

3. Closure: Invite all the retreatants to return to the room. Ask them to comment on their experiences in the dyads.

4:15 p.m. Break

4:30 p.m. Small group 3

Staff: one person for each small group

Purposes: to create a safe atmosphere for the retreatants to discuss the relationships they have with their family members and to provide them with the opportunity to hear about one another's family situations

Materials needed: crayons and an 8½-by-11-inch paper for each retreatant

Description of activities

1. Introduction (10 min.): Invite the retreatants to talk about their reactions to the quiet time and the dyad activity. Ask them to review their goals and the guidelines that are posted on the wall of the small-group room.

2. Activity (20 min.): Give the retreatants each a piece of paper and some crayons. Ask them to draw two pictures that capture their experiences of family. One is to be a picture that expresses how they view their families, and a second picture is to express how their families view them. The time for drawing is meant to be reflective, helping them to get more closely in touch with their family experiences.

3. Discussion (55 min.): Encourage the retreatants to participate in a discussion about "family," using the questions suggested below. Remind the retreatants of the guidelines, if necessary.

• How do you view your family?
• How does your family view you?
• What are ways you feel supported by your family?
• What are areas of tension in your family?
• How can you add to the quality of your family experience?
• What would you like to say to your family members?

The topic "family" is a sensitive one. The retreatants need a safe place to talk about their experiences. This is not meant to be a problem-solving group. Rather, it gives the retreatants an opportunity to articulate their experiences. Often talking about an experience sheds new light on the matter.

4. Summary (5 min.): Encourage the retreatants to continue to respect the confidentiality of the group. Ask if any of them wish to make a closing comment.

5. Closure: Invite a retreatant to lead the group in a closing prayer.

6:00 p.m. Dinner

One staff person is available to make announcements and to choose a retreatant to lead the grace before the meal.

7:15 p.m. Reconciliation

Staff: two leaders and several priests, depending upon the number of retreatants

Purpose: to make available to the retreatants the Sacrament of Reconciliation

Materials needed: a Bible, a small candle for each retreatant, a tape recorder, a tape with appropriate music, an Easter candle, a sandbox (aluminum roasting pan filled with sand), and a lamp (needed if the lighting in the chapel cannot be dimmed)

Description of activities

Place the Easter candle in the center of the room. Give each retreatant a small candle when he or she enters.

1. Opening prayer: "We have gathered for our reconciliation service. Let's begin with a prayer. [Pause.] God of power and mercy, open our hearts in welcome. Remove the things that hinder us from receiving one another and from receiving Christ. We ask this so that we might share in his peace, his mercy, and his forgiveness when he comes in glory. We ask this in the name of Jesus Christ, our Lord, Amen."

2. On reconciliation: "In your small groups you have been talking about relationships. Now is an opportunity to look inside and respond. The word *reconciliation* means 'to restore' or 'to make good again.' This time of reconciliation will be an opportunity to look at your relationships with God, your family, your friends, and yourself and decide what needs to be restored.

"The Sacrament of Reconciliation is a time when we celebrate God's love and mercy. Try to center on the gift of God as truly present in a loving and caring way. This is a time to celebrate God's gift of peace, of special presence. All of us have some aspect of our life that needs to have peace—a part of us that needs to be touched by God's healing. This is a time for that to take place. Be open to this healing. Try to set aside anxiety, fear, worry, and just really celebrate God's love.

"I would like to focus on 'light' as our theme. Please listen to this reading from the Gospel of Matthew." Read Matt. 5:14–16.

3. Examination of conscience: "There are ways that we cover up our light or blow it out. This happens when we choose not to love. This happens when we choose not to restore relationships—when we choose to hold on to fears and anger. What are areas in your relationships with God, your family, your friends, and yourself that keep your light from shining? To assist you in your reflection, I will read a list of questions. Choose one area that really applies to you." Read the questions below slowly.

Regarding myself
- Have I been lazy?
- Have I been impatient?
- Have I been afraid to stick up for what I believe is right?
- Have I been selfish, thinking that my way is the only way?
- Have I hurt myself through habits of smoking or drinking or by eating too much?

Regarding my friends
- Have I been quarrelsome or petty with others?
- Have I been unable to forgive someone who hurt me, even someone I say I love?
- Have I not been open to the ideas or feelings of others?
- Have I failed to say "I'm sorry," especially when I *know* I've hurt another?
- Have I treated others differently because they are of a different race or belief?

Regarding my family
- Have I failed to show love and affection for my family?
- Have I broken promises or otherwise shown that I could not be trusted?
- Have I failed to listen to my parents' words of advice?
- Have I spent most of my time with friends and forgotten my family?
- Have I seen family members in need but didn't come to their assistance?

Regarding God
- Have I not taken time to pray?
- Have I failed to turn to God in moments of loneliness, depression, or anger?
- Have I failed to turn to God during times of happiness and joy?
- Have I turned to God only to *ask* rather than to pray also in thanksgiving?
- Have I been blind to the presence of God in Scripture, in Church, in others, in myself?

4. Extinguishing our light: "We're going to do something symbolic that will help us to see clearly what happens to our light when we choose to do the things on the list I just read. Notice the Christ candle in the center of the room. This is the candle blessed at the Easter Vigil. For ages, light has been a sign of God's presence. So the Christ candle represents Christ's presence with us. Each of you has your own mini–Christ candle. I will light my candle, then I'll light a few of yours. Turn to those next to you and share your light. When all the candles are lit, we will dim the lights. Notice how our small candles still light the room.

"I will then read the list again. When I read the question that applies to you, please blow out your candle and sit down. If none of the questions applies to you, please be seated when I read the last one, which will refer to any other area in your relationships. Please stand."

In silence light the candles.

"Notice how you are able to see one another. Remember the reading from Matthew: 'You are the light of the world.' I will now read the list. Please blow out your candle and sit down at the appropriate time. Darkness will surround us, just as it does when we choose to extinguish our light in relationships."

Read the list a second time. Include the following at the very end: "Have I failed in another way in my relationships with God, family, friends, or self?" As the leader, you may need to keep your candle lit when you sit so that you are able to see your notes. After you have read all the questions, pause in the darkness, then raise the room lights slightly so that you are seen by the retreatants.

5. Confessions: "Only the light of Christ burns. Christ depends on us to be light for the world. I would like to give you the opportunity to restore your light. First, I encourage you to seriously consider receiving the Sacrament of Reconciliation, which is available to you today. Allow the Lord to remind you of the love that is yours. God says 'I love you' through the reminder of the priest. If you choose not to receive the sacrament, perhaps you could ask the priest for a blessing or ask him to pray with you for a particular relationship. After speaking with Father, light your candle again from the Christ candle and place it in the sandbox."

Indicate the priest(s) who will be hearing confessions. If there is more than one priest available for the sacrament, tell the retreatants where each will be located.

6. Reconciling with one another: "While you are waiting to see Father and afterward, I encourage you to move around the room and converse one-on-one with as many people as possible, to offer forgiveness, thanks, or support. Only two people should be together at a time. With more than two, it is difficult to have a very personal conversation. Are there any questions?" Turn on the music. Dim the lights. At the conclusion of confessions, turn the lights up, turn off the music, and gather the group in a circle or direct them to their original seats. Close with the Lord's Prayer.

8:45 p.m. Break

9:30 p.m. Liturgy preparation

See the Appendix, pages 103–107, for a full explanation of the committees and instructions for presenting the session on liturgy preparation to the retreatants.

10:30 p.m. Break

10:45 p.m. Night prayer

Staff: two people

Purposes: to create an atmosphere where the retreatants can reflect on how others have been supportive to them and to provide them with the opportunity to voice a prayer of thanks

Materials needed: a Bible, firewood, matches, a stick for each retreatant and staff member, a tape recorder, and a tape of an appropriate song (e.g., "Thank You for Loving Me" by Tom Franzack)

Description of activities
This prayer takes place in front of a fireplace or around a fire. Light a fire and have a stick available for each retreatant.

"Welcome to our night prayer. Today has been a very busy day. So let's take a few moments to quiet ourselves. [Pause.] As you can see, we have not gathered in the chapel for prayer as we usually do. Prayer can take place anywhere. Jesus said that wherever two or more are gathered in his name, he would be present.

"Our theme tonight is 'thankfulness.' We have spent time on this retreat examining our relationships. We have thought about the people who have influenced our lives. Tonight I invite you to offer a prayer of thanks for a particular person in your life.

"The fire burns brightly and gives warmth and light. The wood provides the fuel and energy so the fire can stay alive. Loving friends and family members are the wood or fuel in our lives. They provide warmth, light, and energy for our lives. The fire consumes the wood, though, just as the love of God consumes us. Think about a particular person while we listen to this song." Play "Thank You for Loving Me" by Tom Franzack.

"There are a few guidelines for tonight's prayer. I invite each of you to come to the fire one at a time and pick up a stick. Hold the stick and offer your prayer of thanks. Then place the stick in the fire. Try to keep a spirit of prayerfulness. Be attentive to one another and join in each one's prayer." Offer the first prayer as a model for the retreatants. Take a stick. Stand facing the group and offer a prayer: "Lord, I thank you for . . ." Place the stick in the fire. Return to your seat. After everyone has had a chance to voice a prayer of thanks, read Sir. 6:14–17 as a closing.

11:15 p.m. Closedown

One staff person explains the schedule for the third day and makes announcements.

Retreat Activities: Day 3

7:45 a.m. Wake-up call

8:00 a.m. Breakfast

8:45 a.m. Cleanup

Staff: one person

Purposes: to instruct the retreatants on the expectations for preparing to depart and to provide the time for them to change sheets, clean rooms, pack, and load the cars or the bus

Materials needed: none

9:30 a.m. Morning prayer

Staff: two people (including one to assist with distributing the materials)

Purposes: to create an atmosphere for the retreatants to reflect on the experience of the retreat and to provide the time for them to write a letter to themselves as a remembrance of the retreat

Materials needed: a piece of stationery, an envelope, and a pencil for each retreatant; a Bible; a tape recorder; a tape of appropriate music (e.g., "Make Love Stay" by Dan Fogelberg); and Handout 8–C, "Dear Me: A Letter of Encouragement"

Description of activities

"The theme for our retreat has been 'Journey.' In many ways we are like the early Christians whose faith in Jesus led them on a journey. One of those people was Saint Paul. He was a person whose faith and response to the Lord led him to many cities. He shared his faith and his experience of Jesus.

"Many times Paul wrote letters to encourage the people he had visited. Even though there was a lot of distance between them, Paul wanted to let them know that he still supported them. Timothy was a young man who received a letter from Paul. At the time, Timothy was about your age. I would like to read from one of Paul's letters to Timothy. Paul was encouraging Timothy to continue the growth that had begun in him, and I wish to encourage you to continue whatever has begun for you during this retreat." Read 1 Tim. 4:12–16.

"Paul wrote that letter because he knew that when Timothy was back on his own, he might need some support to continue to grow. In the same way, I encourage you to continue to grow. Be aware of the gifts that you have. Put them into practice for yourself and others.

"This retreat has been a safe place to be yourself. In this atmosphere it is easier to drop any self-consciousness or pretenses you may have. Soon you will be leaving this experience. What can you take back with you? How can you make the growth continue? What have you learned about yourself? I would like you to take a few minutes to reflect upon that."

Play the song "Make Love Stay" by Dan Fogelberg. "The words of the song talk about being able to make love stay—being able to hold on to the mystery. This morning as a part of the prayer, I ask you to write a letter to yourself as a way of encouraging and reminding yourself about the mystery and the gifts that are yours.

"I will pass out pencils, envelopes, blank paper, and some questions. Take some quiet time to reflect on the questions. Then write a letter to yourself. No one else will see this letter. Seal it in the envelope. Please write your first and last name on the envelope. If you finish your letter before we call you to return to the chapel, simply remain still and reflect on your experience. These letters will be given back to you in about a month. We hope they will be an encouragement to you at that time. Are there any questions? You may remain inside the chapel or find a quiet place to be alone outside."

Pass out pencils, paper, envelopes, and Handout 8–C, "Dear Me: A Letter of Encouragement." Play some instrumental music in the chapel. After fifteen minutes, call the retreatants to return to the chapel. Have a basket available for the letters and boxes for the pencils and the handouts. (The retreat leader should keep these letters for a month and then return them to the retreatants.)

"Let's close our prayer with a blessing from Saint Paul." Read 1 Thess. 3:12–13.

10:15 a.m. Break

10:30 a.m. Small group 4

Staff: one person for each small group

Purposes: to have a discussion about friendship and to give the retreatants the opportunity to affirm one another

Materials needed: none

Description of activities

1. Introduction (10 min.): Invite the retreatants to talk about the night prayer of thanks and the morning prayer of letter writing. Ask them to review the guidelines that are posted on the wall.

2. Discussion (30 min.): Encourage the retreatants to participate in a discussion of friendship, using the questions suggested below. Remind them of the guidelines, if necessary.

- What do you look for in a friend?
- What turns you off in a friend?
- Who is a person who has been a friend to you?
- What is difficult for you in a friendship?
- What is easy for you in a friendship?
- How do your family members treat your friends?

3. Goals (15 min.): Invite the retreatants to state their goals again and to explain whether or not they accomplished them. Ask which activities helped them to achieve their goals.

4. Affirmation (45 min.): Invite the retreatants to speak to each group member about what they appreciate in that individual. Choose one person to begin. All group members in turn speak directly to this person, saying, "I appreciate _____ about you." After everyone has addressed this person, ask if he or she wishes to make a statement to the group. Do this affirmation for each group member.

5. Summary (5 min.): Encourage the retreatants to continue to grow in their relationships with family, friends, self, and God. Thank them for their cooperation.

6. Closure: Invite a retreatant to lead the group in a closing prayer.

12:15 p.m. Lunch

One staff person is available to make announcements and to choose a retreatant to lead the grace before the meal.

1:15 p.m. Liturgy

The committees carry out those parts of the liturgy for which they are responsible.

2:30 p.m. Concretizing

Staff: one person

Purposes: to remind the retreatants of the retreat theme and to challenge them to keep alive any resolutions or commitments made

Materials needed: none

Description of activities

"Please take a moment now to be aware of how you are feeling. [Pause.] You are the person who is responsible for the success of this retreat. If you have had a good experience, then you can thank yourself.

"I challenge you to take home with you whatever you have learned. Home will be the same as when you left. If any change has taken place during the last few days, it is within you. Take with you trust, honest communication, attentive listening, prayer, playfulness, and especially a spirit of reconciliation.

"In a few weeks the letter that you wrote to yourself this morning will be returned to you. Let that letter be a reminder to you of all the good that has taken place within you.

"We will continue to pray for you, and I encourage you to pray for one another. When we began the retreat, you extended a sign of support to others. Now, I invite you to offer one another a sign of thanks."

3:00 p.m. Departure

What to Consider Before the Retreat

The introduction to this manual contains useful information about what to consider in advance of a retreat. The reader is here referred to that material, and specific additions for this retreat are also noted below.

Details in advance: See pages 11–12.

Personnel needed: See page 12.

Agenda for the staff preretreat planning meeting: See page 12.

Materials needed: See page 12.

In addition, for the *liturgy preparation,* bring decoration supplies (crayons, scissors, glue, tape, construction paper, pencils, a ruler, and a large piece of butcher paper) and five Bibles.

For the *reconciliation service,* bring an Easter candle, a small candle for each retreatant, and a sandbox (aluminum roasting pan filled with sand).

The *"People Bingo"* materials needed are a kazoo, a hula hoop, a jump rope, and three tennis balls for juggling.

Miscellaneous materials needed are a candle for the prayer service, firewood and sticks for the night prayer, volume 2 of the *Glory and Praise* songbooks, an envelope for each retreatant, and two small boxes of crayons for each small group.

The handouts that follow should be reproduced in advance, with each handout on its own page.

Directions: In the exercise below there are twenty-five squares, each containing a statement or an activity. The object is to find a person within the group who has had one of the experiences listed or who is able to perform one of the activities.

You may sign your own "bingo card" only once. You may sign as many other papers as you wish, but you may not sign any one individual's more than once.

The first person to completely fill his or her card is the winner.

Can do a cartwheel	Remembers a fairy tale	Can jump rope backwards	Wears contact lenses	Sings very well
Watches soap operas	Can juggle	Can use a hula hoop	Can make an animal sound	Can imitate a TV commercial
Recently got a traffic ticket	Didn't work at all last summer	Is a good dancer ★	Knows the school's phone number	Likes to write poetry
Can whistle "The Star-Spangled Banner"	Plays a kazoo	Has or had a pet turtle	Can play an air guitar	Is a great hugger
Can stand on his or her hands	Has traveled to a foreign country	Can imitate a cartoon character	Knows a clean, funny joke	Can wiggle his or her ears

Directions: The object of the exercise below is to sharpen communication skills. You and your partner will take turns asking questions and listening to the responses of each other as follows:
- Person *A* asks questions and listens to the response of person *B* (10 min.).
- Then the roles are exchanged, and person *B* asks questions and listens to the responses of person *A.* (10 min.). Note: When taking the role of listener, nothing may be said in response to the speaker.
- Finally, persons *A* and *B* freely discuss the questions and responses they shared previously (20 min.).

These questions are meant to be only guides. Feel free to talk with your partner about any question that is of interest to you.

1. How do you feel about the retreat so far?
2. What are some of your strengths?
3. What are some of your limitations?
4. How do you want people to remember you?
5. What is the best thing about being a part of your family?
6. What is the hardest thing about being a part of your family?
7. How do you think your family needs you?
8. In what ways do you show your family that you love them?
9. When was a time when you felt close to God?
10. What role does religion play in your life now?
11. What role do you want religion to play in your life ten years from now?
12. What do you look for in a friend?
13. What relationship has affected you the most?
14. What fears do you have for the future?
15. What hopes do you have for your future?

Dear Me:
A Letter of Encouragement

Please take some time to write a letter to yourself. Allow the letter to be both a remembrance of the retreat and a reminder of all you have learned.

Please *read* and *reflect* on the questions below. They will help you to think about the retreat experience and about how you might incorporate your new insights into your life at home and at school. In the spaces provided, jot down some of your thoughts. Then, on the stationery, include your reflections in the letter that you write to yourself.

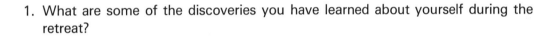

1. What are some of the discoveries you have learned about yourself during the retreat?

2. What new insights have you gained about your own prayer life?

3. How can God become more a part of your daily life?

4. Do you have any expectations for your own growth in the future?

5. Have you made any commitments to develop your relationships with other people?

6. How do you feel about the retreat experience?

7. How do you feel about yourself?

Retreat 9
Parent-Teen Relationships
(Weekend Version)

Retreat 9 ("Parent-Teen Relationships"), described earlier in a two-day, overnight format (Retreat 7), can be expanded into a weekend version, that is, from Friday evening to Sunday afternoon, allowing a somewhat more leisurely pace and more opportunity for informal socializing among the retreatants. Both the overnight version and this weekend version use the same activities and contents, but the weekend retreat offers additional times for prayer, recreation, and meals. And of course, it offers the advantages for the parents' and teens' relationships of being together for the longer period of two nights and two days in a fresh, renewing environment.

To use the weekend schedule, refer to Retreat 7, where the corresponding activities that appear in both retreats are described. Two pieces (besides the additional free time and meals) are added in the weekend version: the night prayer on the first evening and the morning prayer on the second day. These prayers are described following the weekend schedule below. Handout 9–A, "Solitude Questions," also is included for use with the morning prayer. This handout is the only addition to the materials needed for Retreat 7.

Schedule

Day 1

7:00 p.m.	Arrival
7:30 p.m.	Introduction and prayer
8:00 p.m.	Icebreakers
8:45 p.m.	Break
9:00 p.m.	Small group 1—parent-teen partners
10:00 p.m.	Night prayer*
10:30 p.m.	Closedown

Day 2

8:15 a.m.	Wake-up call
8:30 a.m.	Breakfast
9:30 a.m.	Morning prayer*
10:45 a.m.	Small group 2
12:00 m.	Lunch
1:15 p.m.	Recreation
3:00 p.m.	Peer dyads
4:30 p.m.	Break
5:00 p.m.	Liturgy preparation
6:00 p.m.	Dinner
7:00 p.m.	Strength-weakness dyads
9:00 p.m.	Reconciliation
10:30 p.m.	Closedown

Day 3

8:15 a.m.	Wake-up call
8:30 a.m.	Breakfast
9:15 a.m.	Morning prayer
10:30 a.m.	Small group 3—parent-teen partners
11:15 a.m.	Letter writing
12:00 m.	Cleanup
12:30 p.m.	Lunch
1:30 p.m.	Liturgy
2:45 p.m.	Concretizing
3:00 p.m.	Departure

*Additions for the weekend version

Additional Retreat Activities: Day 1

10:00 p.m. Night prayer

Staff: two people

Purpose: to invite the retreatants to offer prayers of hope

Materials needed: a Bible and a candle

Description of activities

"Tonight we gather to pray with the theme of 'hope' as our focus. The Lord offers to each of us a future full of hope." Read Jer. 29:11–15.

"There is a simple structure for this communal prayer. We will pass a candle around the circle. I invite each of you to offer your prayer out loud when the candle comes to you. The prayer could be one of hope for the retreat or for any other concerns you have. If you do not wish to offer a prayer out loud, when the candle comes to you, offer a silent prayer. Please join one another in prayer by listening attentively." Begin by offering a prayer of hope: "Lord, I hope . . ." Then pass the candle until all have had the opportunity to pray aloud.

"Lord, we place our hopes before you. We believe that you hear our prayer and will provide all that we need to live out our future full of hope. We pray this in Jesus' name. Amen."

Additional Retreat Activities: Day 2

9:30 a.m. Morning prayer

Staff: two people (including one to assist with the handouts)

Purpose: to invite the retreatants to reflect on the importance of solitude in their lives

Materials needed: a Bible and Handout 9–A, "Solitude Questions"

Description of activities

"Good morning. Let's begin our day by taking a moment to remember that we are in the holy presence of God. [Pause.] The theme for our prayer this morning is 'solitude.' Often in Scripture we read that Jesus took time to be alone. Listen to this reading from Mark's Gospel." Read Mark 1:35–39.

"Solitude has many advantages: Spiritually, I am able to nourish and tend to my relationship with my Creator. Physically, my blood pressure lowers when I remove myself from the noise and activity. Mentally, I am able to clear my mind and refocus on my values and priorities.

"This morning, I invite you to find a quiet place away from the crowd. Quiet your mind and your body. Allow the Spirit of Jesus to fill you. Take the 'Solitude Questions' with you. However, if you decide not to reflect on those questions, feel free to pursue whatever you need.

"The next activity will not begin until 10:45 a.m., when we meet in small groups. Try to use the next forty-five minutes as a gift of solitude. I now invite you to find a quiet place." Distribute Handout 9–A.

Directions: Find a quiet place where you can be alone to reflect on your spiritual relationship with the Lord.

The questions below are intended to help stimulate this meditation, but you are free to pursue other spiritual reflections.

Rising early the next morning, Jesus went off to a lonely place in the desert; there he was absorbed in prayer. (Mark 1:35)

- When does your weekly schedule allow you to have time to yourself?

- Do you take advantage of this time and use it for personal reflection?

- How could you rearrange your schedule to include time for quiet prayer?

- What gifts do you have that you would like to offer your parent (teen) this weekend?

Retreat 10
Peacemakers

Goals

The retreat "Peacemakers" is designed for older (eleventh- and twelfth-grade) retreatants. It is a three-day program—Friday evening to Sunday afternoon—for twenty-five to forty-five participants.

The goals for the retreat are the following:

1. The retreatants will reflect on passages from the U.S. bishops' pastoral letter on peace.
2. The retreatants will explore their own attitudes toward issues of peace and justice.
3. The retreatants will examine personal behavior and discuss ways to act justly and peacefully.

Schedule

Day 1

7:00 p.m.	Arrival
7:30 p.m.	Introduction and prayer
8:15 p.m.	Icebreakers
9:00 p.m.	Break
9:15 p.m.	Small group 1
10:15 p.m.	Break
10:30 p.m.	Night prayer
11:00 p.m.	Closedown

Day 2

8:00 a.m.	Wake-up call
8:30 a.m.	Breakfast
9:15 a.m.	Morning prayer
9:45 a.m.	Break
10:00 a.m.	Peace activity 1
10:45 a.m.	Small group 2
12:00 m.	Lunch
1:00 p.m.	Organized recreation
1:30 p.m.	Break
2:30 p.m.	Quiet time
3:30 p.m.	Peace activity 2
4:30 p.m.	Small group 3
6:00 p.m.	Dinner
7:00 p.m.	Reconciliation
8:30 p.m.	Break
9:00 p.m.	Liturgy preparation
10:30 p.m.	Night prayer
11:00 p.m.	Closedown

Day 3

8:00 a.m.	Wake-up call
8:30 a.m.	Breakfast
9:15 a.m.	Cleanup
10:00 a.m.	Morning prayer
10:45 a.m.	Break
11:00 a.m.	Small group 4
12:00 m.	Lunch
1:15 p.m.	Liturgy
2:30 p.m.	Concretizing
2:45 p.m.	Departure

Retreat Activities: Day 1

7:00 p.m. Arrival

Two staff members welcome and register the retreatants, help them locate their rooms, and have them fill out name tags.

7:30 p.m. Introduction and prayer

Staff: two people (including one to assist with the handouts)

Purposes: to lead the retreat community in prayer, to introduce the theme of the retreat, to introduce the retreat staff, and to explain guidelines for using the retreat facility

Materials needed: a Bible and Handout 10–A, "Peace Prayer"

Description of activities

Part 1: "Welcome to your retreat. My name is _____. As we begin the retreat, let's remember that we are in God's holy presence." Pause.

"I would like to make a few comments about the nature of your retreat. I will begin by reading a passage from the Book of Deuteronomy. [Read Deut. 30:19–20.] I believe that as Christians we have the responsibility to choose life. This, in the end, will be the way to peace. The focus of this retreat is on how we might become peacemakers. How can we create peace?

"During the retreat you will be given the opportunity to examine your attitudes about peacemaking and your own behavior. Do you think you can make a difference in the world by talking through disagreements with your friends or your parents? In May 1983, the U.S. Catholic bishops wrote a letter, *The Challenge of Peace: God's Promise and Our Response.* You will be given a copy of this pastoral letter. In small groups we will discuss the challenge and invitation given to us by our bishops. The schedule also includes quiet times, playful activities, serious activities, and times for prayer.

"The success of this retreat depends greatly on your cooperation. Be open to the graces that God wishes to share with you. Call upon God frequently to aid you."

Distribute Handout 10–A. "Let's join together now in the 'Peace Prayer.' " Lead the group in reading from the handout.

Part 2: See part 2 of the "Description of activities" on page 14 of Retreat 1 for the introductions and the practical details. At the conclusion, invite the retreatants to the location of the icebreakers.

8:15 p.m. Icebreakers

See pages 75–76 in Retreat 8 and Handout 10–B, "People Bingo," p. 100.

9:00 p.m. Break

9:15 p.m. Small group 1

Staff: one person for each small group

Purposes: to create an environment in which the retreatants feel comfortable to share their thoughts and feelings, to have them set a goal for the retreat, and to facilitate a discussion of the concepts of peace and justice

Materials needed for each small group: four large pieces of butcher paper, a felt-tip marker, masking tape, and a copy of the U.S. bishops' pastoral letter on peace for each retreatant

Description of activities

1. Introduction (10 min.): "I would like to begin with simple introductions. We will go around the circle. As you introduce yourself, please tell us your name and why you chose to come on this retreat. After a person has been introduced, please feel free to respond to the person or ask any question you might have regarding his or her introductory comments." Proceed with introductions. Encourage the retreatants to talk freely about their reasons for attending the retreat.

2. Guidelines (10 min.): "During this retreat we will meet as a small group four times. These discussions are meant to give you a chance to articulate your questions and to expose you to the thinking of others. Before we begin, I would like for you to establish some guidelines. What makes a discussion good? I will write down the guidelines you decide upon. I will hang them up on the wall so we can refer to them if necessary." With the felt-tip marker, write the guidelines on the butcher paper. Make sure the following are included: confidentiality, respect, no put-downs, honesty, and an attempt to participate by all.

3. Personal goals (10 min.): "When you introduced yourself, you spoke briefly about your reason for coming on the retreat. Could you set a goal for yourself for the retreat? The time goes quickly, and it is easy to lose the focus. I will write the goals on a piece of paper and hang them on the wall. At the beginning of each small-group discussion, remind yourself of your goal." Invite the retreatants to talk about their goals. Record these on the butcher paper.

4. Discussion (20 min.): Encourage the retreatants to participate in a discussion of the questions suggested below. If the group is slow to discuss, pair each retreatant with another person for a two-minute dyad on one of the questions. Then return to the group discussion. Make sure the guidelines are observed. Be flexible. If the discussion seems to move in an unexpected direction, be open to the needs of the retreatants. The butcher paper can be used to record answers to the first four questions.

- What is your definition of *peace?*
- What is your definition of *justice?*
- What are some obstacles to peace?
- What are some obstacles to justice?
- When you are urged to act peacefully, how do you feel?

5. Summary (5 min.): "Thank you for trusting one another. Before we finish the discussion, does anyone have a comment to make to the group?" Give everyone a chance to make a closing comment.

6. Pastoral letter (5 min.): Pass out a copy of the bishops' pastoral letter to each retreatant. Encourage them to look it over before the peace activity at 10:00 a.m. the next day.

7. Closure: End with a closing prayer and explain the schedule for the rest of the evening.

10:15 p.m. Break

10:30 p.m. Night prayer

Staff: two people

Purposes: to introduce the retreatants to the importance of communal prayer and to provide the opportunity for the retreatants to offer a prayer of conversion

Materials needed: a candle, a Bible, a tape recorder, and a tape of the song "Remember Your Love" (number 134 in volume 2 of *Glory and Praise*)

Description of activities

Have a candle placed in front of the leader. "Welcome to our night prayer. In Matthew's Gospel, Jesus says, 'If two of you join your voices on earth to pray for anything whatever, it shall be granted you by my Father in heaven' (Matt. 18:19). Tonight we have gathered as a faith community to pray in the name of our Lord Jesus.

"When the U.S. bishops wrote the pastoral letter challenging each of us to be peacemakers, they spoke of the importance of a conversion of heart and mind so that we might enter into a closer relationship with God. The word *conversion* means literally 'to turn around.' We need to turn our hearts around in order to walk toward the Way offered by Jesus.

"I invite you to reflect on areas in your life that prevent you from being a peacemaker. Perhaps you need patience, more understanding, or forgiveness. Reflect quietly as I play a song." Play "Remember Your Love," number 134 in volume 2 of *Glory and Praise*.

"We will now create our own prayer. I will pass the candle around the circle. When it comes to you, please offer a prayer using the formula 'Lord, change my heart . . .' After five people offer their prayers, we will respond with the refrain from the song you just heard. We will then continue with the prayer. After the next five people, we will again sing the refrain."

Teach the refrain from "Remember Your Love." Then begin the prayer saying, for example, "Lord, change my heart so I may be forgiving." After everyone has had the opportunity to pray, read Ps. 19:8–15 as a closing.

11:00 p.m. Closedown

One staff person explains the second day's schedule and makes other announcements.

Retreat Activities: Day 2

8:00 a.m. Wake-up call

8:30 a.m. Breakfast

9:15 a.m. Morning prayer

Staff: two people

Purpose: to provide the retreatants the time to prayerfully reflect on scriptural passages about peace and justice

Materials needed: a Bible for each retreatant; Handout 10–C, "Scriptural Passages on Peace and Justice"

Description of activities

"Good morning. Today's schedule is quite full. I invite you to begin your day by offering it to the Lord." Pause for all to offer a silent prayer.

"Prayer involves speaking as well as listening. Last night we offered prayers asking God to change our hearts so that we might become men and women of peace. This morning I invite you to practice the listening side of prayer. If we are to hear God, then we must take the time to listen.

"As you well know, God speaks to us in a variety of ways—through others, through nature, through our experiences, and through Scripture. We will be using Scripture this morning for our prayer of listening.

"Each of you will be given a list of scriptural passages about peace and justice, along with a Bible. Find a quiet spot where you can prayerfully examine and reflect on these passages. Listen to the voice of the Lord. After twenty minutes, we will gather here for a closing reading. Does anyone have any questions?" Distribute Handout 10–C and the Bibles. At the end of the reflection period, read Ps. 33:1,4–5 as a closing.

9:45 a.m. Break

10:00 a.m. Peace activity 1

Staff: two people

Purpose: to encourage the retreatants to examine the U.S. bishops' pastoral letter on peace

Materials needed: the U.S. bishops' pastoral letter on peace (given to the retreatants the previous night); a pencil and an 8½-by-11-inch paper for each retreatant; Handout 10–D, "Reflections on Peace"

Description of activities

"In May 1983, the U.S. Catholic bishops published a pastoral letter on war and peace. There were two main purposes for doing this. The first purpose was to provide guidance for the Catholic faith community as we form our consciences and make moral decisions. The second purpose was to bring the Church into the public policy debate and thereby influence others in the promoting of human life and dignity.

"This letter was presented in a style that invites Catholics to consider and respond. It is not meant to impose certain ideas on anyone, but it invites us to reflect on the Christian tradition and on Scripture. In light of the data assembled, the bishops made their own best judgment. At the same time, we are asked to examine the information and make *our* own response. This is why we are providing you with the opportunity to read and discuss some of the statements made by the bishops.

"This morning we will examine the section that deals with the religious perspectives on peace and the one that looks at proposals and policies for promoting peace. Later today we will look at the section on the response of the Church. Last night you were given your own copy of the pastoral letter. Now each of you will be given a list of excerpts to read from the letter, a paper, and a pencil. The readings involve a total of about ten pages. After reflecting on these excerpts, write down any questions or insights you might have. In forty-five minutes we will meet in our small groups to discuss what you read. Does anyone have any questions?" Distribute Handout 10–D, "Reflections on Peace"; the pencils; and the papers.

10:45 a.m. Small group 2

Staff: one person for each small group

Purpose: to encourage the retreatants to discuss their insights from peace activity 1

Materials needed: none

Description of activities

1. Introduction (5 min.): Invite the retreatants to review their goals and the guidelines for discussion.

2. Discussion (60 min.): Encourage the retreatants to participate in a discussion of the questions suggested below. Remind the retreatants of the guidelines, if necessary.

- What was your overall reaction to the readings?
- Paragraph 2 – Do you feel hope in the midst of the nuclear threat?
- Paragraphs 11–12 – What is an example of sincere, "faithful" disagreeing on a given matter?
- Paragraphs 14–15 – What are specific ways you can reflect God's presence in the world?
- Paragraphs 46–47 – What are obstacles to forgiveness and love in your life?
- Paragraph 49 – Who in recent history have defended themselves without using force? What are the pros and cons for this?
- Paragraph 53 – Could you live as a "minister of reconciliation"? What would this entail?
- Paragraph 73 – Have you ever had to defend peace in your home or your school? What did you do?
- Paragraph 78 – What is the paradox that Christians face regarding violence and nonviolence?
- Paragraphs 80–83 – Is a war ever just? What are the historical implications?
- Paragraphs 116–117 – Do you know someone who is a nonviolent Christian witness?
- Paragraph 234 – Where do you need to bring justice and peace into your life?
- Paragraphs 235–236 – Are you willing to be a person living out justice, truth, freedom, and love? What will the obstacles be? Be specific.

3. Summary (5 min.): Thank the retreatants for their honesty. Encourage them to continue to examine these ideas about peace on a personal level. Ask them to keep Handout 10–D because it will be used again in peace activity 2. Invite each participant to make a closing comment to the group.

4. Closure: Ask a retreatant to lead the group in a closing prayer.

12:00 m. Lunch

One staff person is available to make announcements and to choose a retreatant to lead the grace before the meal.

1:00 p.m. Organized recreation

Staff: two people

Purpose: to have the retreatants exercise and enjoy themselves as a group (e.g., by playing volleyball games with four teams)

Materials needed: two volleyballs or other recreational equipment

1:30 p.m. Break

2:30 p.m. Quiet time

Staff: two people

Purpose: to introduce the retreatants to the value of taking time for quiet prayer

Materials needed: a Bible

Description of activities

"We are about halfway through the retreat. The schedule is full, and you have been quite busy. I encourage you to use the next forty-five minutes as a time for quiet reflection. Try to refocus and think about your goal.

"Find a comfortable spot where you can relax and be still. Breathe slowly and deeply in order to relax. Let this be a time of renewal." Read Isa. 30:15 to introduce the quiet time.

3:30 p.m. Peace activity 2

Staff: two people

Purpose: to encourage the retreatants to continue their study of the pastoral letter on peace

Materials needed: the U.S. bishops' pastoral letter on peace (given previously to the retreatants), a pencil and an 8½-by-11-inch paper for each retreatant, and Handout 10–D, "Reflections on Peace"

Description of activities

"This activity is similar to this morning's peace activity. The readings we'll be looking at now come at the end of the pastoral letter. As followers of Jesus, the bishops invite us to respond to their challenge. Read the excerpts that are listed on the handout you received this morning and consider carefully the bishops' suggestions. I will give you a pencil and paper if you wish to take notes. At 4:30 p.m., we will meet in our small groups to discuss the readings."

4:30 p.m. Small group 3

Staff: one person for each small group

Purposes: to encourage the retreatants to discuss their reactions to peace activity 2

Materials needed: none

Description of activities

1. Introduction (5 min.): Invite the retreatants to review their goals and the guidelines for discussion.

2. Discussion (60 min.): Encourage the retreatants to participate in a discussion of the questions suggested below.

- What was your overall reaction to the readings?
- Paragraph 276—What are some attachments and affiliations that could prevent you from hearing and following your "authentic vocation"?
- Paragraph 277—What are Christian values? Do you know any "mature" and "exemplary" Christians? Who are they?
- Paragraph 284—What keeps you from having peace in your heart?
- Paragraph 285—What violence do you accept as commonplace?
- Paragraphs 288–289—How could you defend life?
- Paragraphs 290–291—Could you add more prayer to your life? Explain.
- Paragraph 292—What is your experience of devotion to Mary?
- Paragraphs 293–296—What keeps you from praying with Scripture, with your family, and with your parish faith community?
- Paragraphs 297–300—Would you be willing to do penance and fast for peace? How? When?
- Paragraphs 307–308—What profession and lifestyle are you considering for yourself?

3. Summary (5 min.): Thank the retreatants for their honesty. Invite each participant to make a closing comment.

4. Closure: Ask a retreatant to lead the group in a closing prayer.

6:00 p.m. Dinner

One staff person is available to make announcements and to choose a retreatant to lead the grace before the meal.

7:00 p.m. Reconciliation

Staff: one leader and several priests, depending upon the number of retreatants

Purpose: to invite the retreatants to receive the Sacrament of Reconciliation

Materials needed: a small candle for each retreatant, a sandbox (aluminum roasting pan filled with sand), an Easter candle, a tape recorder, and tapes

Description of activities

1. Opening prayer: Give each retreatant a small candle. Have the Easter candle in a significant place with the sandbox near. "We have gathered for our reconciliation service. Let's begin with a prayer. God of power and mercy, open our hearts to welcome you. Remove the things that hinder us from receiving one another and from receiving Christ, the Prince of Peace. We ask that we might share in Christ's peace, mercy, and forgiveness when he comes in glory. Amen."

2. Isaiah on peace: "For us as Christians, the cultivation of peace ought to be a way of life. Please listen as I read from the prophet Isaiah. [Read Isa. 2:1–5.] When we walk in the light of the Lord, the instruments that are used for fighting will then be turned into those that are used to cultivate land to produce food—to cultivate that which nourishes and gives life."

3. Examination of conscience: "You have spent the day reflecting on the pastoral challenge to be peacemakers. This evening I invite you to take the time to reconcile yourself with God and with those around you. Whenever we choose not to make peace, we sin. Even on the smallest levels—with ourselves, our families, our friends, our teachers, and our civil leaders. Often we think we don't make a difference. Yet even our attitudes can make the difference between a peaceful and growthful atmosphere and an atmosphere where peace cannot exist.

"Take time to examine your life. I will read a series of questions to help you." Read the following examination of conscience.

- Have I refused to take time to listen?
- Have I broken promises?
- Have I been afraid to stick up for what I believe is right?
- Have I been quarrelsome or petty with others?
- Have I let fear stand in the way of my relationships?
- Have my words been destructive or reflective of a lack of respect for life?
- Have I been unwilling to forgive someone who hurt me?
- Have I been closed to the ideas and feelings of others?
- Have I failed to say "I'm sorry" when I hurt others?
- Have I treated others differently because they are of a different race or belief?
- Have I failed to take time to pray?
- Have I failed to express the love I feel?
- Are there other areas in my relationships in which I have failed to love?

4. Confessions: "At this time I invite you to approach the priest who is available to hear confessions for the Sacrament of Reconciliation, to pray with you for a particular concern, or to give you a blessing. [If more than one priest is available, indicate their locations.] After you see Father, come to the Easter candle. As a sign of your reconciliation and desire to walk with the Lord, light your small candle and place it in the sand.

"While you are waiting to see Father, go around the room and speak to others. Offer support, thanks, or forgiveness. Music will be turned on in the background and the lights will be dimmed in order to give you a sense of privacy." Dim the lights and turn on the instrumental music.

5. Closing: For a closing, invite the retreatants to form a circle. Join hands and pray the Lord's Prayer.

8:30 p.m. Break

9:00 p.m. Liturgy preparation

See the Appendix, pages 103–107, for a full explanation of the committees and instructions for presenting the session on liturgy preparation to the retreatants.

10:30 p.m. Night prayer

Staff: two people

Purpose: to invite the retreatants to offer a prayer of peace

Materials needed: a Bible, a candle, a tape recorder, and an appropriate tape

Description of activities

"Tonight we gather to pray before we retire. The theme for the prayer is 'hope.' In Scripture, we read that the Lord offers each of us a future full of hope." Read Jer. 29:11–15 and pause for reflection.

"Tomorrow the retreat ends and you will go on your way. Before you go, can you think of what you have learned on this retreat that you would like to integrate into your words and actions? Often when we make resolutions, they only last a few weeks. Tonight in prayer let's ask the Lord to strengthen and assist us in our peaceful resolutions."

During the next few minutes play soft instrumental music for a period of reflection.

"I invite you now to offer a prayer of hope. We will not be going around the circle as we did last night. Simply offer aloud your prayer when you are ready. I invite each of you to participate."

Close by reading Ps. 31:15–17,24–25.

11:00 p.m. Closedown

One staff person explains the schedule for the third day and makes other announcements.

Retreat Activities: Day 3

8:00 a.m. Wake-up call

8:30 a.m. Breakfast

9:15 a.m. Cleanup

Staff: one person

Purposes: to instruct the retreatants on the expectations for preparing to depart and to provide the time for retreatants to change sheets, clean rooms, pack, and load the cars or the bus

Materials needed: none

10:00 a.m. Morning prayer

Staff: two people

Purpose: to invite the retreatants to reflect on the Beatitudes, especially "Blest are the peacemakers . . ."

Materials needed: a Bible for each retreatant; volume 1 of the *Glory and Praise* songbooks; a tape recorder, and a tape with appropriate music (e.g., "It's About Time" by John Denver)

Description of activities

"Good morning! In chapter 5 of Matthew's Gospel, Jesus speaks to the crowds on the mountainside. He teaches them the Beatitudes: 'Blest are the poor in spirit . . . blest too are the sorrowing . . . blest are the lowly.' During this morning's prayer I would like to focus on the beatitude regarding the peacemakers: 'Blest too the peacemakers; they shall be called the sons [and daughters] of God.'

"There are a few comments I would like to make about this passage. First of all, in the Hebrew language, peace means not only freedom from all trouble but also the enjoyment of all good. Secondly, the beatitude refers to *makers* of peace, not *lovers* of peace. And thirdly, that the peacemaker is to be called a son or daughter of God means that the peacemaker is doing God's work. Those who actively make good happen for others are doing God-like work.

"In the song 'It's About Time,' John Denver reminds us that it is about time we all realize that we are in this quest for peace together. We belong to the Family of God. Please listen to this song as a challenge to begin making peace happen now." Play "It's About Time" by John Denver.

"During the next fifteen minutes, I invite you to reflect on Jesus' words—the Beatitudes—in Matthew's Gospel, chapter 5, verses 3–12." Pass out the Bibles.

As a closing, join together to sing "Peace Prayer," number 40 in volume 1 of the *Glory and Praise* songbooks.

10:45 a.m. Break

11:00 a.m. Small group 4

Staff: one person for each small group

Purposes: to invite the retreatants to examine their own behavior in terms of peacemaking and to discuss ways to act justly and peacefully

Materials needed for each small group: an 8½-by-11-inch paper and a pencil for each retreatant

Description of activities

1. Introduction (15 min.): Invite each person to share any reflections from the morning prayer. Ask the retreatants to evaluate the retreat experience by commenting on the prayer services, the peace activities, the small-group discussions, and the schedule.

2. Goals (10 min.): Invite each retreatant to state the goal he or she had for the retreat and discuss whether or not it was accomplished.

3. Resolutions (25 min.): Give each retreatant a pencil and paper. Ask them to write down specific actions they hope to do as a response to the invitation to be a person of peace and justice. Allow five minutes. Have them discuss their resolutions with one other person for five minutes. Then ask the retreatants to share their resolutions with the whole group for fifteen minutes.

4. Summary (5 min.): Thank the retreatants for their honesty and for trusting one another. Ask if anyone has a closing statement that he or she would like to say to the group. Go around the circle allowing each person to make a statement.

5. Closure: Invite a retreatant to lead the group in a closing prayer.

12:00 m. Lunch

One staff person is available to make announcements and to choose a retreatant to lead the grace before the meal.

1:15 p.m. Liturgy

The committees carry out those parts of the liturgy for which they are responsible.

At the introduction to the liturgy, remind the retreatants of the suggestion from paragraph 295 of the bishops' pastoral letter: "The Mass in particular is a unique means of seeking God's help to create the conditions essential for true peace in ourselves and in the world." At the sign of peace, encourage them to make this gesture "an authentic sign of our reconciliation with God and with one another."

2:30 p.m. Concretizing

Staff: one person

Purposes: to remind the retreatants of the purpose of the retreat and to challenge them to keep alive any commitments or resolutions made during the retreat

Materials needed: a Bible

Description of activities

"Please take time to reflect on how you are feeling now. [Pause.] You have worked hard throughout the retreat. If you feel good about this experience, then thank yourself and your fellow retreatants for trusting the staff and fully cooperating.

"I remind you to continue to believe that one person does make a difference. Choose your profession and lifestyle carefully. I also challenge you to continue to examine your behavior and attitudes toward issues of peace and justice. Try to be a reflection of God's loving presence in the world. Love is the hope for the world, and forgiveness makes for an atmosphere of love.

"I assure you that we will continue to pray for you. Please do the same for one another. I would like to close with a reading from Scripture." Read Mic. 6:8, then invite the retreatants to extend a sign of peace to all.

2:45 p.m. Departure

What to Consider Before the Retreat

The introduction to this manual contains useful information about what to consider in advance of a retreat. The reader is here referred to that material, and specific additions for this retreat are also noted below.

Details in advance: See pages 11–12.

Personnel needed: See page 12.

Agenda for the staff preretreat planning meeting: See page 12.

Materials needed: See page 12.

In addition, for *liturgy preparation,* bring decoration supplies (crayons, scissors, glue, tape, construction paper, pencils, a ruler, and a large piece of butcher paper), twenty index cards, and songbooks.

For the *reconciliation service,* bring a sandbox (aluminum roasting pan filled with sand), an Easter candle, and a small candle for each retreatant.

"People Bingo" materials needed are a kazoo, a hula hoop, a jump rope, and three tennis balls for juggling.

Miscellaneous materials needed are a copy of the U.S. bishops' pastoral letter on peace* and a Bible for each retreatant, a candle for prayer, and volumes 1 and 2 of the *Glory and Praise* songbooks.

The handouts that follow should be reproduced in advance, with each handout on its own page.

---

*The Challenge of Peace: God's Promise and Our Response, the U.S. bishops' pastoral letter on war and peace, dated 3 May 1983, may be obtained from the following address:
Office of Publishing and Promotion Services
United States Catholic Conference
1312 Massachusetts Avenue, NW
Washington, DC 20005-4102

Peace Prayer

Lord, make me an instrument of your peace.
Where there is hatred, let me sow love;
Where there is injury, pardon;
Where there is doubt, faith;
Where there is despair, hope;
Where there is darkness, light;
And where there is sadness, joy.

Grant that I may not so much seek
To be consoled as to console,
To be understood as to understand,
To be loved as to love.

For it is in giving that we receive;
It is in pardoning that we are pardoned;
And it is in dying that we are born to eternal life.

Directions: In the exercise below there are twenty-five squares, each containing a statement or an activity. The object is to find a person within the group who has had one of the experiences listed or who is able to perform one of the activities.

You may sign your own "bingo card" only once. You may sign as many other papers as you wish, but you may not sign any one individual's more than once.

The first person to completely fill his or her card is the winner.

Can do a cartwheel	Remembers a fairy tale	Can jump rope backwards	Wears contact lenses	Sings very well
Watches soap operas	Can juggle	Can use a hula hoop	Can make an animal sound	Can imitate a TV commercial
Recently got a traffic ticket	Didn't work at all last summer	Is a good dancer ★	Knows the school's phone number	Likes to write poetry
Can whistle "The Star-Spangled Banner"	Plays a kazoo	Has or had a pet turtle	Can play an air guitar	Is a great hugger
Can stand on his or her hands	Has traveled to a foreign country	Can imitate a cartoon character	Knows a clean, funny joke	Can wiggle his or her ears

Scriptural Passages on Peace and Justice

Please read and prayerfully reflect on the passages below.

Peace: Matthew 5:9
Colossians 3:12–17
2 Timothy 2:22

Justice: Sirach 4:1–10
Matthew 12:16–21
Ephesians 4:17–24

Peace Activity 1

Please read and reflect on the following passages from *The Challenge of Peace: God's Promise and Our Response.*

Introduction—paragraph 2

I. Peace in the Modern World: Religious Perspectives and Principles—
   paragraphs 11–12, 14–15
   A. Peace and the Kingdom
      2. New Testament
         b. Jesus and the Reign of God—paragraphs 46–47, 49, 53
   C. The Moral Choices for the Kingdom
      2. The Presumption Against War and the Principle of Legitimate
         Self-Defense—paragraphs 73, 78
      3. The Just-War Criteria—paragraphs 80–83
      4. The Value of Non-violence—paragraphs 116–117
III. The Promotion of Peace: Proposals and Policies
   B. Shaping a Peaceful World—paragraph 234
      1. World Order in Catholic Teaching—
         paragraphs 235–236

The good Samaritan

Peace Activity 2

Please read and reflect on the following passages from *The Challenge of Peace: God's Promise and Our Response.*

IV. The Pastoral Challenge and Response
   A. The Church: A Community of Conscience, Prayer and Penance—
      paragraphs 276–277
   B. Elements of a Pastoral Response
      2. True Peace Calls for "Reverence for Life"—
         paragraphs 284–285, 288–289
      3. Prayer—paragraphs 290–296
      4. Penance—paragraphs 297–300
   C. Challenge and Hope—paragraphs 307–308

Appendix

Eucharistic Liturgy Preparation for Overnight and Weekend Retreats

Each overnight and weekend retreat provides the retreatants with the opportunity to participate in planning various aspects of the eucharistic liturgy: the decorations, the readings, the music, the offertory gifts, and the Prayer of the Faithful. At the time during the retreat designated for liturgy preparation, the planning committees are explained, and the retreatants choose a committee to work on. A staff member is assigned to assist each committee with its responsibilities. What follows are instructions for the liturgy preparation session, an explanation of each committee's work, and the "Planning Sheet for Eucharistic Liturgy."

Instructions for Liturgy Preparation Session

Staff: a liturgy coordinator and five people, one for each committee, to assist the committees in preparing their parts of the liturgy—readings, music, offertory gifts, Prayer of the Faithful, and decorations

Purpose: to organize the retreatants for their planning of the eucharistic liturgy

Materials needed: ten Bibles, index cards, pencils, music books, and decoration supplies (crayons, scissors, glue, tape, construction paper, pencils, rulers, butcher paper), and the "Planning Sheet for Eucharistic Liturgy" on page 107.

Description of activities

"This is the time that we have set aside to prepare for our closing liturgy. In that liturgy we will come together as a faith community to celebrate that Jesus is present among us.

"Before we begin our planning, I would like to briefly review the main parts of the liturgy. Each eucharistic liturgy begins with a penitential rite. This is a time for us to reconcile with God and one another and to prepare ourselves to better listen to and respond to the Word of God.

"The eucharistic liturgy is then divided into two basic parts: the liturgy of the Word and the liturgy of the Eucharist. During the liturgy of the Word our focus is on *listening*. The Word of God is proclaimed in the readings from Scripture. A homily is given to help us to apply the message of Jesus to our daily lives. After hearing the Word of God, we respond with the Prayer of the Faithful.

"During the liturgy of the Eucharist, our focus is on *sharing*. We prepare the offertory gifts, which are a spiritual expression of our very selves. We then recall the night before Jesus died, and we share in the Bread of Life. After the reception of Communion, the celebrant prays that we might be nourished by the Gift that we have received. And during the concluding rite, we are all sent to do the works of the Lord while praising and blessing God.

"I like to take the time to explain the various parts, because I believe that many people simply tune out what is happening during the eucharistic liturgy. My hope is that you will approach our closing liturgy with fresh eyes and ears. Let the words of the celebrant and the prayers become your own.

"In order to help you participate more fully in this celebration, I would like for you to take the responsibility for various aspects of the liturgy. Five committees will be needed. Consider your interests and your talents, and in light of those, choose a committee that you would like to help. The committees are (1) decorations, (2) music, (3) offertory gifts, (4) Prayer of the Faithful, and (5) readings.

"The decorations committee is responsible for preparing the chapel with artwork, posters, and so on. The decorations are to remind us of our reason for coming together.

"The music committee is responsible for choosing and leading the songs to be used during the liturgy. The music is meant to provide an atmosphere of prayerful celebration. It should be used to enhance the liturgy, not to entertain or to concertize.

"The committee for offertory gifts is responsible for choosing and presenting the offertory gifts that will be brought up with the bread and wine. The gifts are symbolic expressions of our entering into the sacrifice of Christ.

"The committee for the 'Prayer of the Faithful' is responsible for writing and presenting the petitions for the Prayer of the Faithful. This prayer is meant to unite us with the individuals with whom we worship, as well as with people throughout the world.

"The readings committee is responsible for choosing and for proclaiming the scriptural readings. This group is also responsible for briefly introducing each reading with an explanation.

"Are there any questions? . . . Take some time to think about which committee you would like to help."

Allow the retreatants time to select and sign up for a committee. Post a sign-up chart with the name and the location for each committee on it. State how much time is available for the committee to work until the next activity, and ask the committees to go to their respective locations and begin working.

The liturgy coordinator receives the information from each committee, fills in the "Planning Sheet for Eucharistic Liturgy," and acts as a liaison between the committees.

The Work of the Committees

Decorations Committee

This committee is responsible for preparing decorations for the chapel. The decorations can contribute visibly to the whole environment and the whole action. They communicate like silent voices. The decorations are to be used to remind the participants of their reason for coming together.

Responsibilities
1. Brainstorm about ideas for decorations.
2. Decide upon an approach.
3. Prepare the decorations.
4. Choose a retreatant to explain each poster or decoration at the liturgy and to write the explanation on an index card.
5. On an index card, write the name of the person who will explain the posters or decorations and give it to the liturgical coordinator.
6. On the day of the liturgy, arrange the decorations.

Supplies needed: crayons, scissors, glue, pencils, butcher paper, construction paper, and index cards

Suggested images
- Jesus theme: Jesus, followers, people helping others
- Confirmation theme: Holy Spirit, people working with each other
- Vocation theme: family, clergy, religious community, single person
- Conscience formation theme: Jesus, two roads
- Values theme: heart, hands, people, church
- Prayer theme: nature, a person alone, communal praying
- Parent-teen theme: family figures, heart, people talking with each other
- Journey theme: a winding road, footprints with the retreatants' names printed on them
- Peace theme: a dove, Jesus, people helping others, the peace sign, grapes and wheat

Readings Committee

This committee is responsible for choosing and for proclaiming the scriptural readings. Sacred Scripture is central in the celebration of the liturgy. We are nourished by the Word of God. Care should be taken that the Word is proclaimed in such a way that the faithful will hear and understand: the one proclaiming the Word should stand, speak slowly, and read with expression. (Note: *proclaim* comes from the Latin word *proclamare,* meaning "to cry out.")

A brief introduction is given by a retreatant before each reading. A few minutes of silent reflection follow each reading.

Responsibilities
1. Using the suggested readings, list some readings that would fit the needs of this retreat.
2. Choose the readings: the first reading, the second reading (optional), and the Gospel. (The first reading is usually taken from the Jewish Scriptures; the second reading is usually taken from the Epistles in the Christian Scriptures. A nonscriptural reading may be chosen for the second reading.) The music committee will plan the psalm response if it is sung.
3. Write the brief introductions to precede each reading.
4. Choose retreatants to introduce and proclaim the readings.
5. Write the list of the chosen readings and the names of the persons proclaiming each reading on an index card and give it to the liturgical coordinator.
6. Before the liturgy, the retreatants who will proclaim the readings should practice. The staff member will listen for the proper volume and speed and give feedback. The practice of the readings should be done standing.

Supplies needed: Bibles, index cards, and pencils

Form suggestions: The first and second readings begin with "A reading from . . ." and end with "This is the Word of the Lord." The gospel reading begins with "A reading from the holy Gospel according to . . ." and ends with "This is the Gospel of the Lord."

Suggested readings

Jewish Scriptures
Num. 6:22–27 (blessing)
Sir. 2:1–6 (duties)
Isa. 35:1–6,8–9 (deliverance)
Isa. 43:1–7 (I have called you)
Isa. 49:15–16 (God's love)
Dan. 3:52–90 (praise)

Epistles
Phil. 1:3–11 (hope)
Phil. 4:4–9 (joy and peace)
1 Thess. 5:23–24 (blessing)
1 Tim. 6:11–16 (goodness)
1 John 3:1–3 (child of God)
1 John 4:11–16 (God is love)

Gospels
Matt. 5:3–12 (Beatitudes)
Matt. 5:13–16 (light of the world)
Mark 12:28–34 (Great Commandment)
Luke 9:1–6 (mission of the Twelve)
Luke 12:22–31 (God's providence)
Luke 24:13–35 (road to Emmaus)
John 13:33–35 (New Commandment)
John 15:1–8 (vine and branches)

Music Committee

This committee is responsible for choosing the songs, leading the singing, and—if there is musical talent among them—providing instrumental accompaniment. The music is meant to provide an atmosphere of prayerful celebration. The music should be used to educate the retreatants and enhance the liturgy, not to entertain or concertize.

In planning the music, the following must be considered: (*a*) the message or theme of the readings, (*b*) the personality of the worshiping community, (*c*) the potential resources (including the competence and experience of the musicians), and (*d*) the aesthetic balance and beauty.

The parts of the liturgy where music might be used are the following:
entrance procession
responsorial psalm
Gospel acclamation
offertory procession (instrumental)
Holy, Holy, Holy
memorial acclamation
Great Amen
Lord's Prayer
Lamb of God
Communion
Communion meditation
recessional

Responsibilities

1. Brainstorm about the following: What songs do you know? Will the accompaniment be by someone from the staff or by the retreatants? What instruments will be used? Who is willing to sing (solo or part of a choir)?
2. Choose appropriate songs for the different parts of the liturgy. (Not all areas need a song. If the group is relatively small, usually a Communion meditation song is not needed with a Communion song. One seems to be adequate.)
3. Write the list of songs to be used on an index card and give it to the liturgical coordinator.
4. Decide who will introduce the songs, who will be responsible for operating the tape recorder, and who will rehearse the songs with the retreatants.
5. Practice the songs as a committee.
6. Before the liturgy starts, pass out the songbooks and practice the songs with the other retreatants.

Supplies needed: songbooks, paper, pencils, index cards, a tape recorder, tapes with songs, and instruments

Suggestions

(from volumes 1 and 2 of the *Glory and Praise* songbooks)
"All My Days" (Psalm 8)
"For You Are My God" (Psalm 16)
"I Lift Up My Soul" (Psalm 26)
"On Eagle's Wings" (Psalm 91)
"Sing A New Song" (Psalm 98)
"You Are Near" (Psalm 139)

Committee for Offertory Gifts

This committee is responsible for choosing, explaining, and presenting the offertory gifts. The gifts, in addition to the bread and wine, are symbolic expressions of the people's entering into the sacrifice of Christ.

The gifts are prepared and presented in some order of significance. After the gift is presented, an explanation is given of the meaning of the gift.

Responsibilities

1. Brainstorm about the following: What gifts would symbolize the retreat experience or the retreatants themselves?
2. Decide upon the gifts to be offered.
3. Write appropriate explanations of the gifts to be offered.
4. Decide who will present the individual gifts, in what order these will be presented, and who is to give the explanations.
5. On an index card, write the names of the persons presenting gifts and give it to the liturgical coordinator.
6. Before the liturgy, place the gifts with the bread and wine at the back of the chapel.

Supplies needed: index cards, pencils

Suggested gifts: bread and wine, flowers, a candle, a class ring, a volleyball

Suggested explanations

"We offer this bread, gift of the earth, which we shall eat and which will soon be transformed into the Body of Jesus Christ."

"We offer this wine, fruit of the earth, which we shall drink and which will soon be transformed into the Blood of Jesus Christ."

Committee for the "Prayer of the Faithful"

This committee is responsible for writing and presenting the Prayer of the Faithful. This is one of the oldest parts of the liturgy. It is the action that ends the liturgy of the Word. As a response to having heard the message of the Lord, we respond as children of God in trust.

This prayer is intended to unite us with the individuals with whom we worship, as well as with people throughout the world. The petitions that are included in it usually focus on the needs of our civil and church leaders, the sick and the suffering, and the poor. There is also opportunity to pray for our own special intentions.

Responsibilities

1. Brainstorm about possible petitions.
2. Write the petitions.
3. Choose an appropriate form and response (e.g., "For _____, let us pray to the Lord. Lord, hear us.").
4. Decide upon the order in which the intentions will be offered.
5. On an index card, write the names of the persons offering petitions and give it to the liturgical coordinator.

Supplies needed: index cards, pencils

Planning Sheet for Eucharistic Liturgy

Theme: _____ Date: _____

Decorations: _____

Musical accompaniment: _____

Leader of song: _____

Introduction: composed by _____ read by _____

Opening song: _____

First reading: _____ read by _____

Responsorial psalm: _____ antiphon _____

_____ said _____ sung _____

Second reading: _____ read by _____

Gospel acclamation: _____

_____ said _____ sung _____

Gospel: _____ read by _____

Prayer of the Faithful: composed by_____ read by _____

Offertory song: _____

Offertory gifts: _____

presented by _____ explained by _____

Holy, Holy, Holy: said _____ sung _____ version (if sung) _____

Memorial acclamation: _____

_____ said _____ sung_____

Amen: said _____ sung _____ version (if sung) _____

Our Father: said _____ sung _____ version (if sung) _____

Lamb of God: said_____ sung _____ version (if sung) _____

Eucharistic ministers: _____

Communion song: _____

Communion meditation (if any): reading _____ read by _____

song _____

Recessional song: _____

Resources

Books

Anderson, Yohann, comp. *Songs*. San Anselmo, CA: Songs and Creations, 1978.

Buscaglia, Leo. *Love*. New York: Ballantine Books, 1972. On relationships.

Caprio, Betsy. *Experiments in Prayer*. Notre Dame, IN: Ave Maria Press, 1973.

Foley, Leonard. *Signs of Love*. Cincinnati: St. Anthony Messenger Press, 1976. On the sacraments.

Gibran, Kahlil. *The Prophet*. New York: Knopf, 1969.

Glory and Praise, 3 vols. Phoenix: North American Liturgy Resources, 1977–82.

Hayes, Bernard. *Who Is This God You Pray To?* Locust Valley, NY: Living Flame Press, 1982.

Jones-Prendergast, Kevin, ed. *Letters to God from Teenagers*. Cincinnati: St. Anthony Messenger Press, 1979. On prayer.

Lindbergh, Anne Morrow. *Gift from the Sea*. New York: Pantheon Books, 1955. On solitude.

Link, Mark. *You*. Niles, IL: Argus Communications, 1976. On prayer.

Linn, Dennis, and Matthew Linn. *Healing Life's Hurts*. Ramsey, NJ: Paulist Press, 1978. On forgiveness.

Mello, Anthony de. *Wellsprings*. Garden City, NY: Doubleday, 1984. On prayer.

More New Games. Garden City, NY: Doubleday, 1981. For designing icebreakers.

The New Games Book. Garden City, NY: Doubleday, 1976. For designing icebreakers.

Nouwen, Henri J. M. *With Open Hands*. Notre Dame, IN: Ave Maria Press, 1972. On solitude.

O'Connell, Timothy E. *Principles for a Catholic Morality*. New York: Seabury Press, 1978.

Peck, F. Scott. *The Road Less Traveled*. New York: Simon and Schuster, 1978. On relationships.

Reutemann, Charles. *Let's Pray!* Winona, MN: Saint Mary's Press, 1982.

———. *Let's Pray/2*. Winona, MN: Saint Mary's Press, 1983.

The Rites. New York: Pueblo Pub., 1976. The official rites for sacraments of the Catholic Church.

Saint-Exupéry, Antoine de. *The Little Prince*. New York: Harcourt, Brace, Jovanovich, 1971. On relationships.

Sanford, John A. *Between People*. Ramsey, NJ: Paulist Press, 1982. On communication.

Satir, Virginia. *People Making*. Palo Alto, CA: Science and Behavior Books, 1972. On family and relationships.

Shelton, Charles M. *Adolescent Spirituality*. Chicago: Loyola University Press, 1983.

Tilmann, Klemens. *The Practice of Meditation*. Ramsey, NJ: Paulist Press, 1977.

Vanier, Jean. *Be Not Afraid*. Ramsey, NJ: Paulist Press, 1975. On prayer.

Audiovisual Materials

Meditation Program. Saint John's Abbey, Collegeville, MN: Liturgical Press. (A series of three meditations, each containing slides, a cassette, and a script)
Meditation 1—saints, thanksgiving, death
Meditation 2—state, penance, family
Meditation 3—earth, spirit, prayer

Instrumentals

Barry, John. *Out of Africa* (movie soundtrack).
Diamond, Neil. *Jonathan Livingston Seagull* (movie soundtrack).
Grusin, Dave. *On Golden Pond* (movie soundtrack).
Pachelbel, Johann. *Canon in D Major*.
Vangelis. *Chariots of Fire* (movie soundtrack).

Parent-Teen Themes

"Perhaps Love." *Seasons of the Heart*. John Denver.
"Father and Son." *Tea for the Tillerman*. Cat Stevens.
"Cat's in the Cradle." *Verities and Balderdash*. Harry Chapin.
"Teach Your Children." *Four Way Street*. Crosby, Stills, Nash, and Young.

Reconciliation Themes

"Hard to Say I'm Sorry." *Chicago 16.* Chicago.
"Never Gonna Let You Go." *Sergio Mendez.* Sergio Mendez.

Miscellaneous Themes

"Bridge over Troubled Water." *Simon and Garfunkel's Greatest Hits.* Paul Simon and Art Garfunkel.

"Dear Father." *Jonathan Livingston Seagull.* Neil Diamond.

"Ebony and Ivory." *Tug of War.* Paul McCartney and Stevie Wonder.

"Fire and Rain." *Sweet Baby James.* James Taylor.

"The Good Lord Loves You." *September Morn.* Neil Diamond.

"How Can I Tell You?" *Footsteps in the Dark.* Cat Stevens.

"I Just Called to Say I Love You." *Woman in Red.* Stevie Wonder.

"I Will Follow." *Dad Loves His Work.* James Taylor.

"I Wish I Knew How It Would Feel to Be Free." *Best of Nina Simone.* Nina Simone.

"Imagine." *John Lennon Collection* or *Shaved Fish.* John Lennon.

"It's About Time." *It's About Time.* John Denver.

"Know Who You Are." *Famous Last Words.* Supertramp.

"Lord, Is It Mine?" *Breakfast in America.* Supertramp.

"Make Love Stay." *Greatest Hits.* Dan Fogelberg.

"Nobody Loves Me Like You Do." *Heart Over Mind.* Anne Murray.

"On the Road to Find Out." *Tea for the Tillerman.* Cat Stevens.

"On the Wings of Love." *Jeffrey Osborne.* Jeffrey Osborne.

"Shower the People." *In the Pocket.* James Taylor.

"Sometimes." *Carpenters.* Carpenters.

"We Are the World." *We Are the World.* USA for Africa.

"Without Your Love." *Best Bits.* Roger Daltry.

"You've Got a Friend." *Mud Slide Slim and the Blue Horizon.* James Taylor.

Note: In order to stay more aware of the songs that the teenaged retreatants listen to, contact Fr. Don Kimball at Cornerstone Media, P.O. Box 6236, Santa Rosa, CA 95406; phone (707) 542-TAPE. Cornerstone regularly publishes *Cornerstone Review,* a review of popular music, as well as songs adapted from current hits.

Youth Retreats
Creating Sacred Space for Young People

Aileen A. Doyle

Most youth ministers—and many others who work with young people—are so busy that they seldom have adequate time to plan new programs. This manual is for such people. Each program includes outlines, lists of materials needed, sample scripts, and other helpful hints that provide a step-by-step guide for carrying out retreats. The resources that are included are ready to use, and although some of the youth ministers, retreat coordinators, and retreat house personnel who use *Youth Retreats* will be able to adapt it for particular settings, others with less experience will find what is here more than adequate, even for their initial retreat experience with young people.

Designed to meet the current needs and issues of adolescents, the topics of the ten retreats are pertinent to this age-group: relationships (family, friends, God, self), values, communication, prayer, vocations, peace, conscience formation, Confirmation, and parent-teen relationships. Some of these sessions are planned as one-day retreats, while others are intended as overnight or weekend experiences. The approach is holistic; it is designed to integrate the spiritual, physical, emotional, and psychological needs of the retreatants.

Youth Retreats offers a fine checklist of what is needed to assure the smooth running of a retreat. But more than that, *Youth Retreats* is a rich resource of program activities, handouts, and innovative ideas that are both stimulating and practical. Highly recommended for retreat teams as well as for individual retreat directors.
Thomas W. Gedeon, SJ
Executive Director
Retreats International

This book fills a gap in youth ministry resources; it has been long awaited by many youth leaders. *Youth Retreats* is the most complete retreat manual I've seen.
Glenda Carline
Coordinator of Youth Ministry
Archdiocese of Edmonton

Aileen Doyle has made a significant contribution to the lives of youth and youth ministry coordinators with her new resource book, *Youth Retreats*. The result can only be a high satisfaction rate for teens and those who love them. A Winner!
Fr. Don Kimball
Cornerstone Media

Now the benefits of such a well-developed program are readily available to staffs and students anywhere. Anyone with the need and desire to provide a dynamic retreat experience for students can do so with this manual and an adequate physical plant.
Robert J. Randall
Teacher and Campus Minister
Santa Rosa, California

About the Author
Aileen A. Doyle has taught high school religion and math, coached, worked as a college admissions counselor, and coordinated the retreat program in a high school. She is currently assistant program director at the Christian Brothers Retreat House in Saint Helena, California, where along with being a member of the retreat team, she trains retreat staff and coordinates in-service education and program development.

SAINT MARY'S PRESS
Terrace Heights
Winona, Minnesota

ISBN 0-88489-177-1

$12.95

DATE DUE			
MAR 25 1996			
JAN 0 3 2000			
MAY 1 9 2004			
			Printed in USA